MW01657115

Drink Smarter! Beverages

101 delicious, health-boosting, sugar-free lattes, teas, hot chocolates, frozen drinks, yogurt drinks, sodas, mocktails, and infused waters.

CARRIE BROWN

Foreword by Dr. Ted Naiman
Physician and creator of Diet And Exercise 2.0 and Burn Fat Not Sugar

Text and Photography Copyright © 2015 Carrie Brown

All rights reserved.

No part of this publication may be reproduced, distributed, or transmitted in any form or by any means, including photocopying, recording, or other electronic or mechanical methods, without the prior written permission of the author.

Recipes are provided for private and personal use only.

The text and recipes should not be considered a substitute for professional medical advice. The author shall not be held liable for any adverse effects arising from the use of the information and recipes contained herein. The reader should consult a qualified medical professional before starting any new health or diet program.

ISBN-13: 978-1508862536

ISBN-10: 1508862532

DEDICATION

Jonathan Bailor

I would not be where I am today without your influence, Mr. Bailor.

You inspire me, you cheer me on, you believe in me, you're my biggest advocate, and you hug me so hard I think you may have cracked a rib or two.

You gave me wings to fly. You pointed me in the right direction to make best use of my talents and to follow my passion. You shared my work with the world like no one else. You also gave me my fat-control and cholesterol-busting mojo back, and for that I have no words that can adequately express my gratitude.

CONTENTS

Acknowledgements

Foreword

Drink Up! 1

Ingredients & Equipment 5

Recipes: Lattes 13

Recipes: Teas 23

Recipes: Hot Chocolates 29

Recipes: Yogurt & Frozen Drinks 37

Recipes: Sodas, Spritzers, and Mocktails 47

Recipes: Infused Waters 57

Recipe: Sugar-free Marshmallows 73

Where to Get More Cool Stuff 74

Carrie Brown 75

Index 76

ACKNOWLEDGEMENTS

Wildman - for brainstorming ideas from the comfort of my massage chair, endlessly proof-reading the draft and listening to me drivel on about the difficulties of making syrup without sugar, grilling steak and tossing salad when I was too tired to cook, and cheering very wildly from the sidelines. Oh, and exclaiming, "WOW!" a lot when you tasted all these drinks. Taste-tester extraordinaire, enthusiastic embracer of a whole new wellness lifestyle, and a total inspiration in the how-to-radically-change-your-life-in-two-days stakes. You're a gem. Thank you!

Charlie Guthrie – for taking me away from the kitchen for a couple of days to play, and shoot, and eat, and fall over a clump of daffodils and bust my ankle. Great girl times, great girl. Plus, your endless enthusiasm and excitement for my cookbooks is so encouraging and empowering. Thank you!

Dr. Ted Naiman – for your tireless work to help improve people's lives through diet and exercise, for writing a wise and brilliant foreword, and for embracing my work with such enthusiasm. Thank you!

For everyone – that includes you! – who supports me by buying my cookbooks, following my blog, cooking my recipes, and listening to the podcasts...THANK YOU!

You are the reason that I do what I do, and there is no worthier cause.

FOREWORD

Food is the single most important factor in human health.

Humankind is facing its greatest epidemic. One in twelve persons on earth has diabetes. A third of all Americans have pre-diabetes. We are facing a crushing burden of obesity, diabetes, and chronic degenerative diseases including diabetic complications, cardiovascular disease, cancers, and dementia. The common underlying theme of all of this is insulin resistance.

Every single facet of our biology is geared towards optimum survival, and insulin resistance is no exception. In the epic struggle to survive, we have cherished every morsel of nutrition encountered. In times of catastrophe this could easily be the difference between life and death.

Food is information to our bodies. A high amount of digestible carbohydrates is a seasonal nutrient indicator of summertime, to store as much energy as possible for the impending future deprivation of wintertime. We are carefully engineered to deliberately become insulin resistant and store fat under these circumstances. This is not a mistake on the part of Mother Nature.

Unfortunately, humans have developed the ability to manufacture our own food, comprised mostly of refined carbohydrates and industrial seed oils—empty calories which short-circuit our otherwise perfect biology, leading to chronic uncontrolled hyperinsulinemia and a host of associated diseases.

The projections are grim. The current acceleration of obesity and diabetes is overwhelming. This disease tsunami is poised to bankrupt global healthcare and destroy the lives of countless individuals worldwide. Our experts have tried to help, pleading with us to eat less and move more. Studies prove that the vast majority of attempts at dieting are doomed to long-term failure, and exercise does not lead to meaningful weight loss for most of the population. Our campaigns to count calories and increase exercise are abject failures. Modern medicine has promised a pill for every ill since the development of antibiotics, and yet it has completely failed to deliver a panacea when it comes to the entire spectrum of metabolic diseases stemming from our ill-conceived modern diet.

All is not lost! The way forward is bright and clear: we have to completely rethink food and our relationship with food. Real food, whole food, as found in nature, this is the secret— and this secret has been here all along. We need to cherish and respect food, and elevate it to the very highest possible importance. We have to give our bodies what they expect, based on our genetics, and shaped over millennia. When we give our bodies exactly what they need and expect, we communicate a powerful message: all is right with our environment. When we communicate this wonderful news to our bodies, we can begin to expend boundless energy for exercise, exploration, and reproduction. We can fully express our genetics because we are in a nutritionally dense environment. We no longer have to conserve energy, storing excessive fat and minimizing movement.

The most powerful thing that the average person can do to optimize their health is a specific dietary change: maximize the nutrient density of their diet by eating whole, real foods as found in nature—while avoiding refined carbohydrates, industrial seed oils, and other toxins. All we are lacking is knowledge. How do we accomplish this task?

The saviors of our collective health will not be doctors, or obesity researchers, or scientists in a lab. They will be the wonderful people out there who already have the wisdom to equate health with the food that we put inside our bodies. One of these visionaries, a beacon who understands the true importance of food, is Carrie Brown. She has elevated food to the lofty position it deserves. She cherishes food as something quite sacred, to be celebrated with wonder and awe, to be enjoyed and respected. Carrie Brown understands the power food possesses, both for good and for evil.

Thank you Carrie Brown for your tireless devotion to food. May we all reconnect with food the way you have, for only then can our species reverse our downward health spiral and regain our rightful vigor.

Our choice of drink shares equal importance with food when it comes to health and wellness. With this latest edition in a growing series of excellent cookbooks, Carrie skillfully highlights healthy and delicious beverages. In doing so, she teaches us all that the path to wellness can be luscious, decadent, and ambrosial!

Ted Naiman, MD

Physician and creator of Diet And Exercise 2.0 and Burn Fat Not Sugar

DRINK UP!

I didn't intend to write a beverage book. It wasn't even on my radar let alone my to-do list, so it's very odd that not only is it now firmly on my radar, but here I am writing it. A cookbook all about drinks. Hand on heart I had no idea where to even start with these recipes, but I soon discovered that making healthy beverages is a lot easier than you might think. If you're worried that great-tasting beverages must be complicated and difficult to make, rest assured you will be amazed at how simple it is. You'll be a healthy beverage Pro in no time!

Do you ever think about beverages as anything other than a tasty way to get liquid inside you, and a delightful addition to your social occasions? I am not sure anyone thinks much about beverages at all, and I'm certain that most of us don't think about beverages as being food. They just slip-slide down oh so easily, and they don't even fill us up. They don't *feel* like food, so it's like they don't count – especially when we're thinking back to what we ate in a day or are working on ways to get healthier and leaner through the food that we eat. It does not occur to us that most beverages these days do not tell the hormones that tell us we're full, so it is very easy to just drink and drink and drink. Which is fine if it's just water.

We're thirsty, we grab a hot or cold drink and get on with our day. As I was sitting in Starbucks, Sugar-free Caramel Latte (Ugh! Artificial sweeteners and dodgy milk!) in hand, it suddenly hit me that there is a huge gaping hole in my wellness plan, and more than likely most other peoples too. What's missing is delicious beverages that heal and promote health and fat loss. There are plenty of beverages that do the opposite, but very scarce are the few that are actually good for us. What the world needs, I concluded, is delicious beverages that help us reach our wellness goals. Because let's face it, the vast majority of beverages available –plain water aside – are filled to the brim with sugars and / or artificial sweeteners – neither of which help us *in the slightest* towards our health and wellness goals. And despite drinks not *feeling* like food those frou-frou lattes and frappés, cans of soda, and over-dinner-drinks contribute significantly to our daily food intake. I wondered how many of us are inadvertently derailing our ability to reach our wellness and fat loss goals because of what we are drinking.

So I toddled off home and started to experiment with different options for coffee. I began making healthy frou-frou lattes right there in my kitchen, getting all kinds of excited about how simple (and cheap!) it was to make them at home. Then it was just a small leap to try my hand at conjuring up healthy sodas, frappés, hot chocolates...and this whole beverage cookbook idea just exploded from there.

The fantastic news is – you too can transform your daily beverage intake into something super-healthy and super-delicious. Fast, easy, convenient – and cheap. If you buy one frou-frou latte or Frappé a week you'll have saved the cost of this cookbook in under a month and be able to have your yummy coffee and drink it too. Every day if you want. Winning!

The backbone of the recipes in this book are extracts (see page 56 for more details). I use them extensively in the majority of the sections. You may wonder why, so here goes.

Extracts allow you to get a big burst of flavor without the complications that using fresh produce requires, and they allow you to naturally flavor all kinds of beverages without adding any sugars or fats – like fruits or nuts for example – would do. They are quick and easy to use, natural, and easy to store. They don't require any work, and you can use them year round without considering the season. Plus, they are significantly cheaper than using fresh produce. They are the simplest, easiest, and healthiest way to flavor beverages. Extracts allow you to create delicious, healthy drinks at the drop of a hat, and who wouldn't want that?

It is true that I could have used fruits that used to hang on a tree, pure fruit juices, and herbs and spices in their whole state – artisanal beverages if you will. However, I am certain that most of you don't have either the time or the inclination or want the complications of such an approach. Maybe in the future I'll write the artisanal version of this book for those of you who just love playing in the kitchen making extraordinary things. Another issue with using fruit – particularly juices – is their high sugar content, which is the very thing we are trying to avoid in our beverages.

For now I just wanted to get you a whole book full of truly healthy delicious ways to up the ante on your water intake in the fastest, cheapest, easiest, and healthiest way possible. Drinks don't have to be complicated to be awesome, although the internet would have you believe otherwise. I want you to have drinks that are so fast and so simple you'll feel like a drink-making guru and give you a really happy set of taste buds. Not to mention no deleterious effects on your body or waistline.

So what prompted me to make beverages the subject of a cookbook? It's true that drinks and I have a rather tumultuous past. From enraging my mother every single day because I'd leave half-finished cups of liquid all over the house, to my utter distaste for drinking both water and green tea, and front-loading my consumption of alcohol – there was a short period of time where I drank enough of it to last the rest of my life – drinks and I have never really gotten along famously. So it's rather ironic – and a little strange – that I should choose to spend a not insignificant amount of time, energy, and resources writing a book on how to drink more. Or rather, how to drink more without consuming vast quantities of sugar and / or making your taste buds want to move out. Deep down we all know that drinking fluids is critical to our health and well-being, but despite knowing that I had never found the magic trick to get me to do just that.

I very rarely feel thirsty. Ever. I have tried countless times to do the fill-up-a-2-liter-bottle-in-the-morning-and-make-sure-it's-gone-by-bedtime routine, but I just don't think to drink and I have never been inspired to down 2 liters of anything that didn't make my taste buds happy. I also know that I hate drinking plain water, and tea – which is a little odd for a Brit. I tried to learn to love green tea and failed dismally at that. I do like pop, or soda, or whatever you call it in your part of the world, and could drink cans of that stuff every day. I managed to switch from regular soda to diet, knowing that regular soda was slowly killing me, but also knowing that the chemicals and artificial sweeteners in diet drinks weren't much better. I liked drinking coffee but didn't like the effect it had on me, and I stopped drinking alcohol some 24 years ago. Juices are so full of sugar I may as well drink soda.

Add all that up and it doesn't really leave a lot else, except a dizzying array of beverages in the coolers at grocery stores that are almost all just sugar in its various forms masquerading as health tonics. Don't believe me? Spend half an hour reading the labels of all those vitamin waters, kombuchas, 'healthy' sodas (using real cane sugar!) and the like and you'll see what I mean.

Then, as if I needed more encouragement to go down this path, out of the blue a trifecta of liquidy experiences in the space of a couple of weeks started jabbing at my conscious and launched me into full on I'm-going-to-write-a-beverage-cookbook mode. Who knew?

The first thing that happened was that I decided I needed to end my love affair with my Nespresso machine, and coffee in general. Coffee has always posed a dilemma for me when it comes to health. Half the world thinks that coffee is the devil, and the other half thinks it is the answer to life, the universe, and everything. Every day, it seems, I read another article extolling the virtues of this studly bean, followed by another article warning me that my every ailment is undoubtedly caused by this most noxious of plant matter. Both parties seem to be able to espouse science and research papers that prove their claims, and frankly, I have never been able to definitively determine what is right and what is wrong in the whole is-coffee-good-or-bad debacle. What I knew for me was this: coffee is not good for people recovering from Adrenal Fatigue, as the constant stimulation further weakens your adrenal glands. Also true, although this may well be TMI...coffee often makes me run *really* fast to the bathroom. So while I am still entirely undecided whether coffee is from heaven or hell, I do know that it is probably not the best option for me. The decision to quit, however, was a real bummer. I love drinking coffee. I get that whole hug-in-a-mug thing that teas just don't provide. I was just going to have to find a way to get my morning and evening mug hugs somehow else.

Next up, I took a close friend out to an all kinds of swanky restaurant for a slap-up birthday dinner. When our server came over and asked us what we wanted to drink, I just couldn't bear to have a celebratory dinner with just a glass of water on the side. Since neither of us drink alcohol, I smiled my biggest smile and said, "Make us exciting birthday drinks! No alcohol. Just surprise us!" Shortly thereafter two exciting drinks arrived, and they were delicious. Total sugar bombs, but delicious. "Make us exciting pink drinks!" He obliged. They were delicious. Total sugar bombs, but delicious. As we sat there enjoying pink drinks and several courses of divine food, it dawned on me that I had to find a way to make special drinks with no sugar. Everyone deserves delicious, exciting drinks on high days and holidays, but without getting diabetes.

Third was a trip to the ER, involving 3 liters of fluid being pumped into one arm - once they had located a vein that hadn't already collapsed, that is. The term pincushion comes readily to mind.

That little trip wound up costing a smidge under $2500 (THANK YOU, insurance!) so it turned out to be a rather expensive trip to the 'bar' for a drink. I could've thrown a full-on drinks party for 50 of my closest friends and still been ahead. Lying there on the gurney, hooked up to a beeping, puffing, flashing device, swaddled in warm blankets – bunches of tubes poking out from underneath – I was reminded yet again how I drink nowhere near enough fluids and that I *really* need to change that unfortunate state of affairs instead of a jaunt to the local hospital.

As the Universe had kindly served me up 3 problems that revolved around beverages, I took it as a sign. I came to the conclusion that I can't be the only one who struggles to find delicious – and healthy – drinks that aren't full of sugar or chemicals. We all love Starbucks and the fancy, frou-frou cups of stuff we line up and clamor to shell out $4 or $5 a pop for, but deep down we know that it's a sure way to raise our blood sugar to the roof and our waistline ever wider. I opined that I'm not the only one bored of drinking plain water all the time. I bet there is a whole bunch of you out there who would love to have a few special drinks on tap during special occasions or other festivities without compromising your commitment to your health and fat loss.

This cookbook was hard to write because the recipes are so simple. If recipes are not complicated and require a bunch of ingredients or funky directions, they have no value, right? Then, one evening while I was having a super-smart engineer of a friend proofread the sections that I had written thus far, he said, *"I'd buy this book just for the infused water recipes. I'd never be able to come up with all those ideas myself."* Another friend got wildly excited when I told her what was going to be in it. *"I'd buy this book just for the infused water recipes"*, she squealed. Déjà vu.

They reminded me that everyone needs to know where to start, and most people need ideas and inspiration – even for the simple things. Having that all in one place – here in this cookbook – makes it so much easier.

Until I started working on this cookbook I didn't realize just how big a role beverages play in the overall feeling of not being deprived, or rather, since I started consuming the drinks I serve up here I no longer feel like I am missing out in the slightest by only eating the uber-healthy foods that I do. These drinks have completely filled the 'treat' gap for me, and I think they might well do the same for you.

Cheers to your good health!

INGREDIENTS & EQUIPMENT

INGREDIENTS

There's not a lot of weird or hard-to-find ingredients required for making a big old mug or glass of healthy yum, but there are a few that may be new to you – don't panic! – especially if you haven't yet availed yourself of my other cookbooks. With a bit of know-how you'll soon discover that you really don't need the usual suspects in the beverage department – such as sugar – to have a delicious drink in your hand.

Here I've listed – in alphabetical order – some bits and pieces that I thought you might need a little more information on. The ones that are new to you will soon be old, familiar, faithful friends. You may even wonder how you lived without them in your 'fridge or pantry thus far in life.

Chicory Root

If, like me, you have eschewed the studly coffee bean, for whatever reason, and are looking for a fantastic alternative, get yourself some chicory root. I buy ready roasted granules.

Chocolate and Cocoa Powder

100% chocolate is chocolate in bar form that has no sugar in it, and it will say 100% on the wrapper, but it's always best to check the label too. It is too bitter to eat on its own for most people but great incorporated into recipes. I use Ghirardelli 100% chocolate.

When using cocoa powder read the label and make sure that it has nothing in it but cocoa. So many cocoa powders have added sugars lurking in them. UGH.

Citric Acid

This is a preservative which naturally occurs in high quantities in citrus fruits. It is great for brightening the flavor of other ingredients without the citrus taste and is also used to add an acidic or sour taste to foods and drinks. It is used extensively when canning or otherwise preserving foods. It is widely available and is sold as a white powder. Look for it where you find herbs and spices, or where canning supplies are sold.

Where a recipe calls for citric acid – especially in sodas – you *really* need it to get the right flavor. Don't skip it. Really. Don't skip it!

Coconut Milk

Thick – this is full-fat, very thick, comes in a can, and solidifies in the 'fridge. It is sometimes called coconut cream. It is made from coconut meat, and is very high in very healthy fats, especially MCTs (Medium Chain Triglycerides). I won't bore you with the technical details of MCTs – just know that they are extremely good for you. Thick coconut milk helps create a smooth and creamy texture. You can use thick coconut milk to replace the heavy (double) cream in these recipes if you want or need dairy-free or vegan versions.

Make sure that you buy it unsweetened, and shake the can very well before you open it. You can find it in most grocery stores and it is often located with the Asian and / or Indian foods. I used Thai Kitchen Unsweetened Coconut Milk for the recipes in this book.

Thin – this comes in a carton and is thin like cow's milk, but is very white. It does not become thick when cold. Make sure you buy it unsweetened. I used Trader Joe's Unsweetened Coconut Milk Beverage for the recipes in this book that call for it.

In a pinch you can use them interchangeably in these recipes if you have one type on hand and not the other. The flavor and consistency of the final drink will be different to that intended, but nothing *terrible* will happen. If you have thick and need thin, you could dilute some thick with water to give a thinner consistency and reduce the richness. If you have thin and need thick, you'll end up with a thinner consistency with less body to it. The world won't end, although your taste buds might not be quite as happy as they could be.

Dandelion Root

Dandelion root is another fabulous roasted root that makes a terrific cup of brew, if you can't or won't do coffee. I buy ready roasted granules so I don't have to do that step myself.

Erythritol – see page 10

Extracts and Flavors (see pages 2 and 56 for further info)

Extracts are the backbone of this cookbook. You will see that I use extracts extensively for the beverages herein – see page 2 for the why.

All those different coffee concoctions with wild and intoxicating names that you can get at coffee houses around the nation are pretty much just coffee with different flavored syrups added, and sodas too are essentially flavored syrups mixed into carbonated water – both with a humongous quantity of sugar thrown in for good measure. Using extracts gives you all the wild and intoxicating without the sugar. Can I get a yippee?!

Once you have your selection of extracts on hand you can use them throughout this cookbook and in a myriad of baked goods and other recipes too. Once you get going you'll become an extract expert!

As you start to explore the world of extracts and flavors you'll see the possibilities are endless. It's important to understand the difference between the two though, since they are not always interchangeable.

Make sure that your extracts and flavors are made with natural ingredients – flavors tend to hide a lot more artificial junk in them than extracts – so just read the labels. For detailed info on the whole *'natural'* thing head over to page 56 – I expect you'll be surprised and pleased by what you read there. Good brands in the US are www.SavorySpiceShop.com and www.OliveNation.com.

Extracts (may be called essences) – these are oils extracted out of fruits, nuts and other foods usually using alcohol. They are very concentrated and can be used to flavor all sorts of things. As they have an alcohol and water base they will disperse easily in water. I almost exclusively use extracts in these recipes, not flavors. Ensure they have an alcohol or water base.

Flavors – these are oils from fruits, nuts and other foods in an oil base. They are also very concentrated and can be used to flavor all sorts of things, however, because they are oil-based they cannot be used in water-based recipes like the beverages in this cookbook.

Follow accurately the quantities in the recipes! Extracts are extremely concentrated and a very little goes a very long way. If you find that you need a stronger flavor afterwards, add in ⅛ tsp. amounts.

Green Tea / Matcha

Green tea is recognized as one of healthiest things you can drink. It can be bought either loose leaf or in tea bags. The taste varies wildly and depends on the quality of the green tea leaves. Buy the best quality you can to fit your budget.

Matcha is finely milled or fine powder green tea. When you drink Matcha you are consuming the entire leaf, not just the brewed water of the infused green tea leaf, so one serving provides the same health benefits as 10 bags of green tea leaves. Buy the best quality you can to fit your budget. The better the quality the better the taste.

Heavy (Double) Cream

I use a splash of heavy (double) cream in some of these drinks because it imparts a particularly smooth and creamy texture, as well as an extra richness of flavor. I don't recommend you leaving it out just in order to lower the fat content. We love healthy fats – they're good for us and we need them. If you need to leave it out to make the recipe dairy-free or vegan, replace the heavy (double) cream with thick coconut milk. The taste and texture will not be the same, but it will be close.

When buying cream I recommend that you look for one that has no added ingredients. If you can find organic cream with no hormones or antibiotics, which is produced by grass-fed cows, so much the better.

Look for heavy (double) cream that does not say UHT on the carton. UHT cream has been treated at ultra-high temperatures to give it a long shelf-life, but that heating also destroys the flavor, and the flavor is half the fun. If heavy cream gets as far as my 'fridge, it won't be there for long, so I never really understood why cream would need a long shelf-life.

Herbs

Herbs are important. Really important. They are little powerhouses in the flavor department of life. Don't leave the herbs out because you think herbs are small and insignificant. Like spices, herbs can have a completely transformative effect on the flavor of even the dullest dish, or in this case, drink. When you try some of these recipes you'll see what I mean. Herbs in drinks? You bet my Mason jar drink dispenser I use herbs in drinks!

In the US the best source for dried herbs is www.SavorySpiceShop.com.

I got annoyed enough by the price of store-bought fresh herbs that I started a little herb garden on my terrace. Not only was it fun to see stuff grow, and oh-so-handy having a never-ending supply of fresh herbs right outside my kitchen door – at least in the Spring, Summer, and Autumn (Fall) months – but it saved me a veritable fortune. Each herb start cost me $1.25 – less than half the price of just a couple of sprigs of fresh herbs from the store – and those starts kept me in herbs for the entire season.

Top tip #1: I planted the herb starts in pots so that they were contained and didn't overrun the entire garden.

Top tip #2: Want your herb garden on steroids? Water them with coffee, dandelion, or chicory grounds. Herb rambunctiousness will abound in your garden. You have been warned.

Juices

The body responds to juices in the same way it does to all forms of sugar, and that's not good at all. You won't find much juice used in these pages, but for the few recipes that call for it ensure that you buy unsweetened juice, and preferably not made from concentrate. Pure, unadulterated and unprocessed is best. It will likely cost a little more but you're worth it.

Milks

Cow's milk is not the healthiest option in the dairy department because of the sugar it contains, but depending on where you are in your health and fat loss journey, or how your taste buds feel about nut milks, you may prefer to use it anyway. For my taste buds, there's nothing quite like full fat cow's milk, but I typically use nut milks for the greater health benefits. Do what works for you. There are several choices of nut milks if you choose to forego or cannot tolerate dairy.

If you use cow's milk I recommend using full fat (whole), non-homogenized milk because it is a much better option nutritionally and also tastes a whole lot better than milk that has had some or all of the fat removed.

If you choose to use nut milk there are several choices: almond, hemp, cashew, and coconut being the most readily available (at least in the US). When buying nut milks the most important thing is to make sure it is unsweetened, and secondly that it is not crammed full of other ingredients. You'll be amazed at some of the things that manufacturers throw in the carton along with the good stuff. Read the label and pick the best of the bunch.

My latest trick for coffees is to use ¾ nut milk and ¼ heavy (double) cream. None of the sugar but a creaminess and body that nut milks just don't have. Plus it froths better. YUM.

While we're talking about milks, I strongly recommend that you stay well way from soy milk (can be very challenging to your hormones – especially for men), rice, oat and any other milk made from grains. Stick to the nut milks and you'll be golden.

Sea salt

Salt is used to brighten and intensify the flavors of beverages, and the right amount of salt can transform things from blah to brilliant. Sea salt stops foods tasting flat. Sea salt has an improved flavor and a higher concentration of minerals than normal table salt, so I highly recommend using sea salt instead of the regular stuff. Salt is also brilliant at reducing bitterness and taking away the tart tang in things like Greek yogurt, but without making them taste salty. There's a lot of funky science behind why it has these magical powers but all I really care about, and all you need to know, is that it does. Salt is awesome. So don't be tempted to leave the sea salt out of the recipes. Salt is important.

Spices

Spices, like herbs, are fabulous. They can perk up a perfectly ordinary dish and turn it into something pretty darn special. Cardamom in your coffee? Yes, please! It adds a delicious, gentle flavor that really hits the spot. Who knew a little dash of cardamom could make hot drinks all kinds of magical?

I typically buy my spices in small amounts, as I need them, from a store that sells them loose, rather than buying pre-packaged jars that I may not use up before they go stale and lose their potency. Spices sold in jars are also significantly more expensive than buying loose. Store your spices in air-tight glass containers, and keep them in a cool, dark place. Heat and sunlight will adversely affect the flavor and potency of the spices. Trust me on this one: use fresh spices. In the US the best source for a huge range of incredibly fresh spices is www.SavorySpiceShop.com.

Sweeteners

If you don't like, cannot tolerate or can't find erythritol or xylitol, then use a non-sugar, zero-calorie, natural sweetener of choice in an appropriate amount. **I do not recommend artificial sweeteners of any kind.** Stevia is popular but I can't vouch for how these drinks will turn out as I have never used it – I hate the taste. Be warned that all stevia is not the same – check for other added ingredients. For PURE stevia use ¼ tsp. for every 1 TBSP xylitol or erythritol.

Xylitol / Erythritol

Many of the drinks in this cookbook use xylitol or erythritol to replace the sugars. If you are new to my cookbooks and blog over at www.carriebrown.com, a few words of explanation will help.

Xylitol and erythritol are the natural sweeteners that I use instead of sugar, because sugar makes you fatter faster than anything, and I'll hazard a guess that you don't want to drink stuff that makes you fatter. They have the same bulk and sweetness as sugar, but are sugar alcohols which are not digested in the same way as other sugars are. They are safe for diabetics as they have a negligible glycemic load. A few people may experience slight intestinal discomfort when they start eating xylitol, but with regular consumption this goes away – don't ask me how I know. For the handful of folks who cannot tolerate xylitol I recommend that you use erythritol, although you do have to be careful and read labels because many erythritol-based products have forms of sugar or other ingredients mixed in.

For detailed information on why I indicate xylitol *or* erythritol in some recipes and specify only erythritol in others please read page 72. There's a really good reason behind everything that I do. Everything. Method in my madness? Yes.

The xylitol brand I use for the recipes in this book is Xyla, because it is made with 100% hardwoods (typically birch bark), and not corn. I do not recommend xylitol that is made with corn. Xyla is non-GMO.

The erythritol brand I use for the recipes is Emerald Forest which is non-GMO.

Both readily available online, and are increasingly available in grocery stores. I buy them in bulk because I get through so much in recipe development that it is a lot cheaper per pound that way. You could start a xylitol / erythritol co-op!

Dog owners please note: like chocolate, xylitol is dangerous to dogs and cats – do not let them share your xylitol-containing goodies!

Yogurt

Buying yogurt is a minefield. If start reading labels you will be stunned at what goes into so many of them. The most dismal and horrifying thing is the amount of sugar they contain. Many flavored yogurts (and some unflavored!) have more sugar than ice cream, while others even have more sugar than a can of soda. And yogurt is supposed to be 'healthy', right?!

The most important part of buying yogurt is reading the label. Compare them all and find the yogurt with the least sugar. Whether you buy whole or 2% or fat-free yogurt depends on what your goals are, where you are in your health journey, and what your taste buds prefer. I use whole unsweetened yogurt.

You can also use Greek yogurt - typically lower in sugar and higher in protein. If so, you may want to add a pinch of sea salt to the recipes to reduce the extra tart that Greek yogurt brings.

EQUIPMENT

In the equipment department, there's a few things that help beverage-making along, and some of them may be new-to-you tools. You do not need to go out and buy these – you can make do with what you already have in your kitchen – these just make the process easier.

French Press

If you don't have an espresso machine or percolator, or you are brewing things other than coffee – such as leaves, spices, dandelion, or chicory – I highly recommend a French press for making your drinks. Super simple to use and clean, inexpensive (depending on the brand), and you can use them to steep all sorts of things instead of using a saucepan (pan).

Frother

Used to create froth for lattes, cappuccinos, hot chocolates and other hot drinks, you can get electric frothers that warm the milk at the same time and hand held frothers that require you to heat the milk separately. The handheld frothers are cheap and work brilliantly. In fact, my handheld frother makes much better foam than my fancy Nespresso machine electric frother so that's what I use now. A good handheld frother can also whip small batches of heavy (double) cream to avoid having to get a machine out and dirty. Totally wish I'd got a frother years ago!

Latte Jug

A stainless steel jug that is wider at the bottom than the top and has a pointy spout designed for pouring and creating latte art. Totally not essential if you like froth on your beverages, but it does make frothing less messy, and if you do want to learn latte art a special jug does make it easier and give you better results than a regular jug.

Measuring Cups and Spoons

I am calling these out here for the non-Americans or anyone else among us who may not use the cup system for measuring ingredients. Those of you who have used my recipes previously will know that I am vehemently against using cups to measure dry ingredients – for accurate and consistent results you need to weigh them. However, I *highly* recommend that you avail yourself of a set of measuring cups before embarking on the recipes in this book. Since most of the ingredients used are liquids, the cup system makes truly light work of measuring everything out. For the odd amount of solid ingredients used, the accuracy of weighing is not crucial to the recipes success, except where specifically called out in the recipe. Truly – get yourself a set of measuring cups. You will thank me. If you just cannot bring yourself to get a set, then you can use the fluid ounce measurements on a measuring jug instead. When it comes to ice, use the measuring jug in the same way where 1 cup = 8 fl. oz.

Measuring spoons – for everything from ⅛ teaspoon to 1 tablespoon are important, particularly when measuring extracts. Extracts are extremely concentrated and even a little too much can ruin a recipe. I recommend not guestimating with extracts. Start with the amount in the recipe and add extra in ⅛ teaspoons if necessary once you have tasted the drink. This is important.

Muddler

A staple in the world of cocktail-making and bartending, a muddler is used like a pestle to mash – or muddle – fruits, herbs, and / or spices in the bottom of a glass to release their flavor. If you don't have a muddler you could use the handle of a wooden spoon or something similar.

Other Equipment

I also have on hand:

- Blenders – I have both a Vitamix and a regular blender. Frappés do better in a Vitamix or similar high-powered blender (although they will work in a regular one), while lassis are fine in a regular blender.
- Chopping boards
- Electric kettle – easily get your water to the right temperature.
- Knives
- Julienne peeler (for making things look pretty)
- Microplanes (for zesting)
- Saucepans (pans) – small and large
- Sieves – fine mesh for straining, tiny, small and large
- Whisks – small, medium, large

~~~~~~

For more info on the ingredients and equipment that I use and love, head over to

WWW.CARRIEBROWN.COM

and in the menu bar

STORE ---> KITCHEN STORE ---> INGREDIENTS and / or STORE ---> KITCHEN STORE ---> EQUIPMENT.
~~~~~~

LATTES

The recipes in this chapter can be made either with brewed coffee or with brewed dandelion and / or chicory roots, so they can be used by those of us who drink coffee as well as those of us who prefer to use an alternative to get that delicious, steaming, hug-in-a-mug.

Dandelion and Chicory Roots

Living in the coffee capital of the world, as I do, I feel really naughty even suggesting that you could even think about using something other than coffee for your brew, but if you can't or don't do coffee, then dandelion and chicory are your new best friends.

I searched high and low through the pile of ready-made coffee alternatives available and couldn't find one that didn't have grains in it. Many of them also used chicory in their blends so I started from there and then discovered dandelion. Both are available as ready-roasted granules so you can simply brew them like ground coffee. Winning!

I got even more excited when I researched the health benefits they have and lo and behold dandelion especially is a veritable wonder plant. I would need 10 pages to list out all the nutrients it has and all the ills it has been credited with improving. Even if you're good with coffee, you might want to incorporate some dandelion and chicory goodness into your life.

These roasted roots are also a lot more economical than coffee as you only use 2 tsps. per cup which works out to be a little more than a third of the cost of one Nespresso coffee pod and gives you your cup of Joe for around 27 cents (US).

It's worth nothing that chicory has a stronger flavor than dandelion, and is a little bitter. Adding a pinch of salt to your brew will help out with any bitterness. A good trick to know for coffee that's on the bitter side, too.

Brewing

There are a variety of ways to brew coffee, so just use your favorite method. For the dandelion and chicory root option there are two main ways to brew – either of which work as well as the other so choose whatever works best for you.

French Press – Boil the water and pour over the roasted root granules in the French Press jug. Stir or swirl well and put the plunger into the jug without depressing it. Leave to brew for 4 minutes. Slowly press the plunger to the bottom of the jug and immediately pour the brew into your cup.

Pan option #1 – Boil the water in a pan on the stove top. Using a mesh tea ball, place the roasted roots in the water and remove the pan from the heat. Leave to brew for 4 minutes. Remove the mesh tea ball with the granules in and pour the brew into your cup.

Pan option #2 – Place the roasted root granules in a pan with cold water. Bring the water to the boil and immediately remove from the heat. Leave to brew for 4 minutes. Pour the brew into your cup through a fine sieve to catch the granules.

Preparing the milk

You can, of course, just enjoy your coffee black or with a splash of cream. Adding a tablespoon or two of either butter or coconut oil is also a great way to incorporate some healthy fats into your day. If you try the butter or coconut oil options I suggest using a hand blender or handheld frother to blend it well as this improves the taste, texture, and appearance.

However, I don't know about you but there is just something about froth that makes hot coffee and chocolate drinks so much yummier and more comforting. I do love a latte. Who knew a bunch of bubbles could make such a difference to a cup of Joe? Not to mention how much prettier and more appetizing they look. Appetizing is important.

Whichever milk you decide to use – cows or nuts (see ingredient section on page XX), the milk must be warmed in order for it to froth well. Frothing will not happen if the milk is either cold or too hot. If you do not have an electric frother but are using a handy-dandy handheld one, either warm the milk in a microwave, or heat the milk slowly in a pan over a low heat so that it doesn't get hot, burn, or form a skin. I touch the tip of my little finger to the surface of the milk to test the temperature and once it is warm remove from the heat. I found that if I start to heat the milk on low once brewing has begun it is warm at the same time as I pour the brew into the cup.

Pour the warm milk into a latte or other jug and froth until it is thick and at least doubled in volume. Gently bang the jug several times on the counter to burst the biggest bubbles and then swirl the jug to mix. Pour the frothy milk into your brew, and then loll in a comfy chair enjoying your perfect homemade latte yum. I cannot tell you how excited I was when I started making lattes at home. So long, SBUX. So long, sugar, artificial flavors, and who knows what else.

If you're already exhausted just reading about brewing coffee and frothing milk at home yourself, then you can relax. Once you've done it a couple of times and realize how easy (and fast) it is, there'll be no looking back. Your body and your wallet will both thank you. A lot.

Frothing notes for cow's milk: not all cow's milk froths the same, and while I could write an entire book on the science and frothing of milk, I'll just give you the cliff notes:

0% (skimmed) cow's milk produces the biggest volume and most stable foam, followed by 2% (semi-skimmed) and lastly whole milk, which can be all kinds of finicky in the frothing department.

0% (skimmed) cow's milk has the least flavor and body, followed by 2% (semi-skimmed) and lastly whole milk, which produces the best texture, body and taste.

Temperature makes a difference to the volume and stability of foam, increasing both up to 100°and then decreasing at temperatures higher than that. The short story – warm is good for foam, too cold or hot is not.

Heated milk tastes sweeter than cold milk because the lactose becomes more soluble as the milk is heated. Bear this in mind when adding your sweetener of choice.

Flavored Lattes

If all those magical sounding concoctions at the coffee shop make you feel like there is some huge mystical secret to making fabulous flavored lattes that only baristas know the answer to, and that you are doomed to shelling out $4 every time you want one, you've been misled. It's only the marketing that is magical. If you hop on up to Starbucks website and check out their menu you'll see that it's pretty much coffee, flavored syrup, and milk. Done. It seems like they have a gazillion different drinks on offer – and they do – but at the end of the day the only difference is the flavor of the syrup.

All of this fancy frou-frou latte-making is in reality so simple and easy that I feel like I'm cheating on you. Once you have tried out a few of these flavor combinations I am sure you'll be creating your own favorite flavors in no time. I am just in love with the idea that I can make super-healthy, exciting lattes right here in my own kitchen. In fact, it must be time for one right now. Be right back.

I started out just brewing dandelion and chicory with water and adding frothy milk, just like I did with coffee. I was amazed at how similar it was in taste to coffee. But it was when I made my second cup and added some vanilla extract that I could be heard exclaiming, "Wow. If I didn't know, I'd think I was drinking a Vanilla Latte from Starbucks! Except this tastes better!"

The next thing I tried was adding my favorite spice to the mix. A Cardamom Latte sounded like my idea of heaven. It was. And despite the myriad of interesting flavors I have downed since this whole crazy latte-making started, this is still the one that heads out the door with me every morning on the drive to work. Thus, it is entirely fitting that is the inaugural latte recipe I offer up to you.

These recipes are so simple and easy to make because no one has time – first thing in the morning as you are running for the door – for all the complicated, time-consuming, sugar-laden latte recipes around the web. You are about to discover how truly easy, delicious, and healthy lattes can be when you get past all the hype and clever marketing.

Let the scrumptious, healthy latte-making begin!

~~~~~~
~~~~~~

Cardamom Latte

- 1 cup / 8 fl. oz. boiling water
- 1 tsp. roasted dandelion root
- 1 tsp. roasted chicory root
- pinch of sea salt
- ½ tsp. ground cardamom
- Xylitol or erythritol (or sweetener of choice – see page 9)
- ½ cup / 4 fl. oz. milk of your choice (see ingredients page 8)

Brew together water, dandelion, chicory, sea salt, and cardamom following instructions on page 13 **OR** brew 1 cup / 8 fl. oz. coffee, add sea salt, ground cardamom and stir well.

Pour into cup and add sweetener to taste.

Heat the milk until it is warm but not boiling and froth per the instructions on page 14. Pour frothed milk into brew.

Cinnamon Roll Latte

- 1 cup / 8 fl. oz. boiling water
- 2 tsp. roasted dandelion root
- ¾ tsp. cinnamon extract (ground cinnamon does not dissolve so you get a gritty drink)
- ¾ tsp. vanilla extract
- Xylitol or erythritol (or sweetener of choice – see page 9)
- ½ cup / 4 fl. oz. milk of your choice (see ingredients page 8)

Brew together water, dandelion, cinnamon and vanilla extracts, and follow instructions on page XXX **OR** brew 1 cup / 8 fl. oz. coffee, add cinnamon and vanilla extracts and stir well.

Pour into cup and add sweetener to taste.

Heat the milk until it is warm but not boiling and froth per the instructions on page XX. Pour frothed milk into brew.

~~~~~~

The next recipe – Black Cherry Amaretto Latte – was inspired by my favorite before-I-got-healthy ice cream. It was terrible for my body, but oh-so-comforting for my brain. This flavor combination just makes my taste buds sing.

Needless to say this Black Cherry Amaretto Latte just hits the spot when I have a craving for something sweet and sinful but don't want the accompanying blood-sugar spike or gallons of insulin pumped around my body. Because, you know, that just leads to fat storage, and why have that when you can get the same taste without? PS. Yes, I will be creating Black Cherry Amaretto Ice Cream. Subscribe to my blog over at www.carriebrown.com to get it!
~~~~~~

Black Cherry Amaretto Latte

- 1 cup / 8 fl. oz. boiling water
- 1 tsp. roasted dandelion root
- 1 tsp. roasted chicory root
- pinch of sea salt
- ½ tsp. cherry extract
- ½ tsp. almond extract
- Xylitol or erythritol (or sweetener of choice – see page 9)
- ½ cup / 4 fl. oz. milk of your choice (see ingredients page 8)

Brew together water, dandelion, chicory, sea salt, and cherry and almond extracts following instructions on page 13 **OR** brew 1 cup / 8 fl. oz. coffee, add sea salt, cherry and almond extracts and stir well.

Pour into cup and add sweetener to taste.

Heat the milk until it is warm but not boiling and froth per the instructions on page 14. Pour frothed milk into brew.

Salted Caramel Latte

- 1 cup / 8 fl. oz. boiling water
- 1 tsp. roasted dandelion root
- 1 tsp. roasted chicory root
- ½ tsp. caramel extract
- ½ tsp. sea salt
- Xylitol or erythritol (or sweetener of choice – see page 9)
- ½ cup / 4 fl. oz. milk of your choice (see ingredients page 8)

Brew together water, dandelion, chicory, caramel extract, and sea salt following instructions on page 13 **OR** brew 1 cup / 8 fl. oz. coffee, add caramel extract and sea salt and stir well.

Pour into cup and add sweetener to taste.

Heat the milk until it is warm but not boiling and froth per the instructions on page 14. Pour frothed milk into brew.

~~~~~~

I pretty much love anything salted caramel. Every Fall I would wait excitedly for the Salted Caramel Hot Chocolate to arrive at Starbucks. I'd ceremoniously let myself have just one, knowing as I do the hormonal disaster it creates in my body. The problem? The caramel syrup. Now all of us Salted Caramel lovers can get our fix without a grain of sugar in sight. Hurrah!
~~~~~~

Peppermint Mocha Latte

- 1 cup / 8 fl. oz. boiling water
- 1 tsp. roasted dandelion root
- 1 tsp. roasted chicory root
- 1 tsp. unsweetened cocoa powder
- pinch sea salt
- ¼ tsp. peppermint extract (this stuff is *very* strong!)
- Xylitol or erythritol (or sweetener of choice – see page 9)
- ½ cup / 4 fl. oz. milk of your choice (see ingredients page 8)

Brew together water, dandelion, chicory, cocoa powder, sea salt, and peppermint extract following instructions on page 13 **OR** brew 1 cup / 8 fl. oz. coffee, add cocoa powder, sea salt, and peppermint extract and stir until cocoa powder is dissolved.

Pour into cup and add sweetener to taste.

Heat the milk until it is warm but not boiling and froth per the instructions on page 14. Pour frothed milk into brew.

Raspberry Truffle Latte

- 1 cup / 8 fl. oz. boiling water
- 2 tsp. roasted dandelion root
- ½ TBSP unsweetened cocoa powder
- 1½ tsp. raspberry extract
- ½ tsp. chocolate extract
- Xylitol or erythritol (or sweetener of choice – see page 9)
- ½ cup / 4 fl. oz. milk of your choice (see ingredients page 8)

Brew together water, dandelion, cocoa powder, and raspberry and chocolate extracts following instructions on page 13 **OR** brew 1 cup / 8 fl. oz. coffee, add cocoa powder and raspberry and chocolate extracts and stir well.

Pour into cup and add sweetener to taste.

Heat the milk until it is warm but not boiling and froth per the instructions on page 14. Pour frothed milk into brew.

~~~~~~

Like a raspberry truffle melted into your coffee, only without the raspberry truffle. Does it get any better than that? I was pretty much born eating fresh raspberries off the canes in my father's garden. I never did get over that. Raspberry love is deeply embedded in my heart. So combine their flavor with chocolate and then drink it? Oh. My.
~~~~~~

Almond Mocha Latte

- 1 cup / 8 fl. oz. boiling water
- 2 tsp. roasted dandelion root
- ½ TBSP unsweetened cocoa powder
- ½ tsp. almond extract
- pinch sea salt
- Xylitol or erythritol (or sweetener of choice – see page 9)
- ½ cup / 4 fl. oz. almond milk

Brew together water, dandelion, cocoa powder, almond extract, and sea salt following instructions on page 13 **OR** brew 1 cup / 8 fl. oz. coffee, add almond extract and sea salt and stir well.

Pour into cup and add sweetener to taste.

Heat the milk until it is warm but not boiling and froth per the instructions on page 14. Pour frothed milk into brew.

Gingerbread Latte

- 1 cup / 8 fl. oz. boiling water
- 1 tsp. roasted dandelion root
- 1 tsp. roasted chicory root
- ⅛ tsp. ground ginger
- pinch ground cloves
- ⅛ tsp. cinnamon extract
- ½ tsp. caramel extract
- ½ tsp. vanilla extract
- 2 pinches sea salt
- Xylitol or erythritol (or sweetener of choice – see page 9)
- ½ cup / 4 fl. oz. milk of your choice (see ingredients page 8)

Brew together water, dandelion, chicory, ground ginger, ground cloves, cinnamon, caramel and vanilla extracts, and sea salt following instructions on page 13 **OR** brew 1 cup / 8 fl. oz. coffee, add ground ginger, ground cloves, cinnamon, caramel and vanilla extracts, and sea salt and stir well.

Pour into cup and add sweetener to taste.

Heat the milk until it is warm but not boiling and froth per the instructions on page 14. Pour frothed milk into brew.

Pumpkin Spice Latte

- 1 cup / 8 fl. oz. boiling water
- 1 tsp. roasted dandelion root
- 1 tsp. roasted chicory root
- pinch sea salt
- Xylitol or erythritol (or sweetener of choice – see page 9)
- ½ cup / 4 fl. oz. milk of your choice (see ingredients page 8)
- 1½ TBSP pumpkin puree
- 1 tsp. vanilla extract
- ⅛ tsp. ground allspice
- ¼ tsp. ground cinnamon

Brew together water, dandelion, chicory, and sea salt, following instructions on page 13 **OR** brew 1 cup / 8 fl. oz. coffee, add sea salt and stir well.

Pour into cup and add sweetener to taste.

Heat the milk, pumpkin puree, vanilla extract, ground allspice and ground cinnamon until it is warm but not boiling and froth per the instructions on page 14 or blend in a blender until frothy. Pour frothed milk into brew.

No Nutella Nutella Latte

- 1 cup / 8 fl. oz. boiling water
- 2 tsp. roasted dandelion root
- ½ TBSP unsweetened cocoa powder
- 1 tsp. hazelnut extract
- 2 pinches sea salt
- Xylitol or erythritol (or sweetener of choice – see page 9)
- ½ cup / 4 fl. oz. milk of your choice (see ingredients page 8)

Brew together water, dandelion, cocoa powder, hazelnut extract, and sea salt following instructions on page 13 **OR** brew 1 cup / 8 fl. oz. coffee, add cocoa powder, hazelnut extract and sea salt and stir well.

Pour into cup and add sweetener to taste.

Heat the milk until it is warm but not boiling and froth per the instructions on page 14. Pour frothed milk into brew.

~~~~~~

Nutella ingredients: sugar, palm oil, hazelnuts, cocoa, skim milk, whey (milk), lecithin as emulsifier (soy), vanillin (an artificial flavor). Still want to eat it? Yeah, me either.
~~~~~~

Coconut Cream Latte

- 1 cup / 8 fl. oz. boiling water
- 1 tsp. roasted dandelion root
- 1 tsp. roasted chicory root
- pinch sea salt
- 1 tsp. coconut extract
- Xylitol or erythritol (or sweetener of choice – see page 9)
- ⅓ cup / 2½ fl. oz. thin coconut milk
- 4 TBSP thick coconut milk

Brew together water, dandelion, chicory, salt, and coconut extract following instructions on page 13 **OR** brew 1 cup / 8 fl. oz. coffee add sea salt, and coconut extract and stir well.

Pour into cup and add sweetener to taste.

Heat the thin and thick coconut milks until warm but not boiling and froth per the instructions on page 14. Pour frothed milk into brew.

Vanilla Rose Latte

- 1 cup / 8 fl. oz. boiling water
- 2 tsp. roasted dandelion root
- 1 TBSP rose water
- ¼ tsp. vanilla extract
- pinch sea salt
- Xylitol or erythritol (or sweetener of choice – see page 9)
- ½ cup / 4 fl. oz. milk of your choice (see ingredients page 8)

Brew together water, dandelion, rose water, vanilla extract, and sea salt following instructions on page 13 **OR** brew 1 cup / 8 fl. oz. coffee, add rose water, vanilla extract and sea salt, and stir well.

Pour into cup and add sweetener to taste.

Heat the milk until it is warm but not boiling and froth per the instructions on page 14. Pour frothed milk into brew.

~~~~~~

I love the flavor of rose. It's likely something to do with the fact that the scent of roses is like crack to me, inducing a delightful, mild euphoria that can leave me contented and peaceful for hours. Rose water is a sweet, subtle flavor that I urge you to try if you haven't. It takes quite a lot of it to overcome the flavor of the coffee or dandelion blend, but it's oh so worth it! This is my mellow-afternoon-cuppa-on-the-couch-with-Mr. McHenry (the cat) latte.
~~~~~~

TEAS

The reputed health benefits of green tea abound. Everything from helping regulate glucose levels in the blood, reducing LDL cholesterol, being anti-viral and anti-bacterial, protecting brain cells, and reducing blood pressure, to reducing the signs of aging. Not to mention its reported ability to reduce tooth decay, kill cancer cells, help depression, and protect against clot formation. Green tea should pretty much come wrapped in a cape, not a bag.

But the reason that green tea got its name put up in lights lately is because of its unique fat-burning effect. Drinking water alone allows our bodies to burn fat far more effectively, but add polyphenol-packed green tea and you can supercharge that. Since I am not the scientist in this outfit, please feel free to take any insatiable quest for hard-core green tea knowledge to the web to get all the scientific studies and research you could ever want. I am just here to share some ideas on how to get your daily green tea fix, especially if you find it as distasteful as I do. Or maybe now I should say *used to do*.

Jonathan Bailor – author of The Calorie Myth – recommends drinking 10 bags of green tea per day to maximize all the benefits that green tea has to offer. Whoa. That's a lot of green tea. One way to do this is to brew all 10 bags (decaf if you prefer) in a small amount of hot (not boiling) water in one go, let it brew for a few minutes, then remove the bags and drink it. You can even add ice to make a cold drink if you prefer it that way over hot. See! 10 bags is easy peasy! The other way to get your 10 bags worth is to drink Matcha green tea instead. 1 teaspoon of Matcha is the equivalent of 10 brewed bags. Of course, all of this is goodness IF you like drinking green tea. Ah. Yes. The big IF.

I hate the taste of green tea. I've tried to like it, so many times. I've forced it down anyway, so many times. No matter how hard I tried, I just hate the taste of green tea. And no matter how good something is for you – and boy is green tea good! – if you can't stomach the taste, it's really hard to get it down.

I know I am not alone in my distaste, so a couple of things you can do instead are to add other flavors to your green tea such as lemon juice (this also provides Vitamin C which makes the healthy compounds in green tea easier to absorb – winning!), or adding some sweetness in the form of xylitol, erythritol, or stevia. The other trick that avoids you having to drink it altogether is especially for you smoothie drinkers out there. Simply add the contents (the leaves themselves) of 3 or 4 bags of green tea into your Green Smoothie when you blend it. You won't be able to taste the green tea but you'll get all the benefits of drinking 10 bags worth. Hurrah!

But here's my Big! Green! Tea! Discovery! that I made a while back. Here's the thing that made me love green tea. Yes! Love as in I-look-forward-to-my-green-tea-every-day-now: Peppermint. I love peppermint herbal tea, and a little while ago while I was musing on my green tea problem yet again, I found myself wondering what would happen if I brewed my peppermint tea with my green tea. Voila! A miracle occurred at the Brown house! I found that by brewing 4 bags of green tea with 1 or 2 bags of peppermint tea and a dash of xylitol in one large mug, I have a drink that I truly enjoy. My struggle with green tea is over. I make a couple of mugs of that a day and I'm all done. You might find a different ratio works better for you, or you might find an herbal tea other than peppermint that you love works better for your taste buds. Do whatever floats your boat, but if you struggle with drinking regular green tea, I urge you to give this a go. It transformed my green tea consumption overnight. Green tea for President!

Top tip: You will retain more of the healthful properties of green tea if you use 175 degree water to make it rather than boiling water. Also, if you use too hot water you will "burn" the leaves and it will taste bitter. So you can either boil your water and then let it cool before you pour it on your leaves, or, if you have the same kettle as I do you can push the magic button that says "green tea" and get water at the perfect temperature. Once my water is the right temperature I steep the bags for only 2 minutes – I actually use a timer so I don't leave them too long – because over-steeping in hot water can also result in bitterness.

You can also cold-brew green tea overnight to further reduce the chance of bitterness, and in the section on Green Tea Frappés later (page 41) I cold-brew a large jug of green tea and keep it in the 'fridge so that I have some cold green tea on hand whenever the mood for a Green Tea Frappé strikes, which is often.

There are other ways to enjoy green tea though and I have included some recipes for you to try in this section, along with some black tea and no tea recipes too.

Chai Tea Latte

- 1 cup / 8 fl. oz. 175 boiling water
- 1 tsp. ground cinnamon
- ¼ tsp. ground allspice
- ½ tsp. ground ginger
- 2 teabags black tea
- 1 TBSP erythritol (or sweetener of choice – see page 9)
- 1 cup / 8 fl. oz. milk of your choice (see ingredients page 8)
- 2 TBSP thick coconut milk

Brew together water, cinnamon, allspice, ginger and tea bags following instructions on page 13. Steep for 4 minutes.

Pour into cup and add erythritol to taste.

Heat the milk and the thick coconut milk until warm but not boiling and froth per the instructions on page 14. Pour frothed milk into brew.

Ginger Tea

- 2 cups / 16 fl. oz. / 1 pint water
- 1" cube of fresh ginger, peeled and chopped
- 4 cloves
- 1 whole star anise
- 1 TBSP erythritol (or sweetener of choice – see page 9)

Place water, ginger, cloves, and star anise in a pan and bring to the boil. Turn heat to low, cover the pan and let simmer for 40 minutes. Uncover, turn heat up and bring back to the boil. Let boil for 5 minutes.

Strain, pour into cup and add erythritol to taste.

Green Tea with Cardamom and Cinnamon

- 2 cups / 16 fl. oz. / 1 pint hot (not boiling) water
- 1 green tea bag
- ½ tsp. cardamom seeds
- 1 cinnamon stick
- 1 TBSP erythritol (or sweetener of choice – see page 9)

Brew together hot water, tea bags, cardamom seeds, and cinnamon stick following instructions on page 13. Steep for 2 minutes.

Strain, pour into a cup and add erythritol to taste.

Raspberry Mint Iced Tea *(picture page 26 top left)*

- 2 cups / 16 fl. oz. / 1 pint boiling water
- 3 mint tea bags
- ½ cup fresh raspberries
- ¼ cup fresh mint leaves
- 1 TBSP erythritol (or sweetener of choice – see page 9)

Brew together water and mint tea bags for 4 minutes, remove the tea bags and then leave to get cold.

Add the cold tea, raspberries, mint leaves, and erythritol to a blender and blend until mint leaves are finely chopped.

Leave the tea to stand for 10 minutes while the tea separates from the froth and raspberry / mint solids. Scoop the froth off with a spoon, then pour the tea over ice through a fine sieve.

Herb Matcha Iced Tea *(picture page 26 top right)*

- ¼ cup fresh mixed mint, tarragon and basil leaves
- 1 tsp. Matcha powder
- 1 TBSP erythritol (or sweetener of choice – see page 9)
- Ice to fill a cocktail shaker or jar
- 1½ cups / 12 fl. oz. cold water

Put the fresh herbs in a cocktail shaker or jar and use a muddler (or similar) to crush them.

Add the Matcha powder, erythritol, and then fill almost to the top with ice.

Add the cold water, and shake vigorously for 30 seconds and then strain into an ice-filled glass.

Matcha Mint Tea *(picture page 26 bottom left)*

- ½ tsp. Matcha powder
- 20 fresh mint leaves, roughly chopped
- 1 TBSP erythritol (or sweetener of choice – see page 9)
- 2 cups / 16 fl. oz. / 1 pint hot water

Place the Matcha powder, chopped mint leaves, and erythritol into a jug and pour on the hot water, stirring well.

Leave to brew for 2 minutes and the strain through a fine sieve into a cup.

Pomegranate Iced Green Tea with Lemon *(picture page 26 bottom right)*

- ½ cup / 4 fl. oz. water brewed with 4 green tea bags, left to get cold
- 1 TBSP lemon juice
- 1½ TBSP unsweetened pomegranate juice
- ¼ tsp. ginger extract
- 2 TBSP erythritol (or sweetener of choice – see page 9)

Add the cold brewed green tea, lemon juice, pomegranate juice, ginger extract, and erythritol into a jug and stir vigorously until erythritol is dissolved.

Pour into an ice-filled glass and garnish with a lemon slice and pomegranate seeds.

~~~~~~

Consuming a teaspoon of Matcha is like drinking 10 bags of brewed green tea, so to get huge amounts of that fat-burning, anti-oxidant-filled, detoxification, and disease-preventing goodness into your body, Matcha is your best friend.
~~~~~~

Chai Indian Tea

- 2 cups / 16 fl. oz. / 1 pint water
- ⅛ tsp. ground cinnamon
- ¼ tsp. ground nutmeg
- ¼ tsp. ground cardamom
- ⅛ tsp. ground cloves
- ½ tsp. ground ginger
- 1 tsp. dried mint
- ½ cup milk of your choice ((see ingredients page 8)
- 2 teabags black tea
- Erythritol (or sweetener of choice – see page 9)

Place water, all the spices and the mint in a pan, bring to the boil and boil for 3 minutes.

Add the milk and teabags, bring back to the boil and boil for another 2 minutes until golden brown.

Strain into a cup, add xylitol or erythritol to taste and serve immediately.

Top Tip: If you drink this often you can make up a large batch of the spice mixture in advance and then use 1¼ tsp. of mixed spices per 2 cups / 16 fl. oz. / 1 pint of water.

Hibiscus Tea

- 2 cups / 16 fl. oz. / 1 pint boiling water
- 1 TBSP dried hibiscus flowers
- 1 cinnamon stick
- 1 TBSP erythritol (or sweetener of choice – see page 9)
- 1 small orange, sliced
- Ice

In a jug, pour the boiling water over the hibiscus flowers and cinnamon stick and steep for 20 minutes.

Strain the tea into a clean jug, add the erythritol, and the orange slices and stir well.

Pour the tea over ice and serve.

Note: longer steeping is not better. For a more intense flavor add more hibiscus and cinnamon.

~~~~~~

I had no idea dried flowers were so delicious until I fiddled with hibiscus petals. I could drink this tea every day and never get bored. It's bright, it's vibrant, and it's full of flavor. Just try it!
~~~~~~

HOT CHOCOLATES

This is the part of the book where we all get to drink something that just seems so wrong but tastes so, so right. Thought you could never indulge in a beautiful mugful of thick, steaming hot chocolate and improve your health at the same time? Come on in!

Chocolate and Cocoa

Chocolate and cocoa (unsweetened, of course) are two of the heathiest things you can eat. Seriously. It's when you start adding milk and sugar and other stuff that it all starts going sideways. The unadulterated versions = dietary awesomeness. In fact, you could say that after water, cocoa is the healthiest known substance you can put into your body. A bold claim? I'll let you head up onto the interwebs and type in 'health benefits of cocoa' so you can read all about it yourself. My job here is to give you some healthy and delicious ways to get it into your body. I am not the scientist in this outfit.

I said it in the Ingredients section but I'll say it again just to be sure we're on the same chocolatey wavelength. 100% chocolate is chocolate in bar form that has no sugar in it, and it will say 100% on the wrapper, bit it's always best to check the ingredients. It is too bitter to eat on its own for most people but great incorporated into hot chocolate. I use Valrhona 100% chocolate when I am feeling rich, and Ghirardelli 100% chocolate ~~the rest~~ of the ~~time~~ most of the time. When choosing cocoa powder read the label and make sure that it has nothing in it but cocoa. So many cocoa powders have added sugars lurking in them – you'll be amazed when you start checking the ingredients lists.

There's a selection of hot chocolate recipes here ranging from the stand-your-spoon-up-in-it rich, thick kind you get in a Parisian café to a couple of spice-up-your-life ones. Try them all! And then, when you're in the mood to feel completely spoiled, float sugar-free marshmallows (recipe page XX) or add whipped cream to the party. Needless to say all of the recipes are sugar-free and healthier than you can even believe.

Talking of sugar, don't be alarmed at the amount of sweetener added – remember that the chocolate and cocoa powder have no sugar in so you need to compensate for that via xylitol or erythritol (or if you prefer stevia you can use that – just check the label for nasties. Not all stevias are what you think they are).

After trying these recipes you will never want to drink 'regular' hot chocolate again.

Taste bud exploding, guilt-free nirvana has arrived in your mug.

GHIRARDELLI

Hot Chocolate like You've (probably) Never Had Before

- 2 cups / 16 fl. oz. / 1 pint water
- 1 oz. / 30g unsweetened cocoa powder
- 1 can / 13 fl. oz. thick coconut milk
- 2 oz. / 55g xylitol or erythritol (or sweetener of choice – see page 9)
- 2 oz. / 55g 100% unsweetened chocolate, chopped

Place the water and cocoa powder in a pan over medium heat until it starts to steam.

Whisk well until the cocoa is completely dissolved.

Add the thick coconut milk and the xylitol or erythritol and stir well. Heat until it starts to steam.

Turn off the heat and add the chopped chocolate, stirring until completely melted and mixed through.

~~~~~~

I should likely warn you that this is some seriously rich, thick, creamy hot chocolate goodness. If you've ever been to Paris and had Chocolat Chaud – think *that* – and you'll know what to expect. If you're used to the watery, faintly-chocolate-tasting liquid that comes out of mixing a powdered mix with hot water, then you're in for a real surprise, or shock, depending on how you look at it.

This incredibly healthy hot chocolate is not for the faint of heart. It is also not for those of you who like a huge ol' mug full of warm beverage. This recipe makes enough for 4, because a small cup of this at one sitting is enough chocolate for the most die-hard chocolate fanatic. There should be a law surrounding the minimum required chocolate y ness of hot chocolate, and I'll leave you to guess which ones I would ban as unsuitable for human consumption. This most definitely would not be one of them.

It's true that there's nothing inventive about hot chocolate, but sometimes just making the classics healthy is enough; no wheel-reinvention required. If you want you can make this whole recipe and then heat up just enough for 1 cup at a time, keeping the rest in the 'fridge. I like doing that {much} better than fiddling with saucepans and fractions of cans of coconut milk every day. You could even just have a cup of this instead of dessert.

<u>Hot Chocolate Love:</u>

Marygrace – *"Best hot chocolate I've ever had. Made it yesterday when I saw the recipe. OMG!! Yum……thank you for this taste of the Gods."*

Alvin – *"It was a hit at the house!! The wife says it's the best she's ever had."*

Karen G – *"Wow, this is really chocolatey. My husband absolutely loves it!"*
~~~~~~

Vanilla Cinnamon Hot Chocolate

- 1 cup / 8 fl. oz. milk of your choice (see ingredients page 8)
- ½ cup / 4 fl. oz. water
- ¼ cup / 2 fl. oz. heavy (double) cream
- ½ TBSP unsweetened cocoa powder
- 1 tsp. ground cinnamon
- 2 tsp. vanilla extract
- 2 TBSP xylitol or erythritol (or sweetener of choice – see page 9)
- pinch of sea salt
- ½ oz. / 15g 100% unsweetened chocolate, chopped

Place the milk, water, cream, cocoa powder, cinnamon, vanilla extract, xylitol or erythritol, and sea salt in a pan over medium heat, whisk well and heat until it starts to steam.

Turn off the heat and add the chopped chocolate, stirring until completely melted and mixed through.

While it is still in the pan, whisk the hot chocolate using a handheld frother or immersion blender for several minutes until it is completely smooth and frothy.

NOTE: the cinnamon will give this a slightly grainy feel as it does not fully dissolve in hot liquid.

Creamy Peppermint Hot Chocolate

- 1 cup / 8 fl. oz. unsweetened almond milk
- ¼ cup thick coconut milk
- 1 tsp. peppermint extract
- 2 TBSP xylitol or erythritol (or sweetener of choice – see page 9)
- pinch of sea salt
- 1 oz. / 30g 100% unsweetened chocolate, chopped
- spoonful of whipped cream
- grated unsweetened chocolate to sprinkle

Place the almond milk, thick coconut milk, peppermint extract, xylitol or erythritol, and sea salt in a pan over medium heat until it starts to steam.

Turn off the heat and add the chopped chocolate, stirring until completely melted and mixed through.

While it is still in the pan, whisk the hot chocolate using a handheld frother or immersion blender.

Pour into mug, add a spoonful of whipped cream and sprinkle grated chocolate over the top.

Oh yeah.

Cardamom Hot Chocolate

- 1 cup / 8 fl. oz. water
- ½ cup / 4 fl. oz. thick coconut milk
- 1½ TBSP unsweetened cocoa powder
- 2 TBSP xylitol or erythritol (or sweetener of choice – see page 9)
- pinch of sea salt
- 1 tsp. vanilla extract
- ½ tsp. ground cardamom

Place the water, thick coconut milk, cocoa powder, xylitol or erythritol, sea salt, vanilla extract, and ground cardamom in a pan over medium heat until it starts to steam, whisking well to dissolve the cocoa powder.

Remove from the heat and while it is still in the pan, whisk the hot chocolate using a handheld frother or immersion blender, then serve.

~~~~~~

Top tip: you could get all fancy and use vanilla pods and cardamom seeds infused in the liquid, but because chocolate is such a strong flavor you lose the flavor nuances that the seeds and pods provide, so I recommend saving yourself the time, trouble and expense and using vanilla extract and ground cardamom instead. You won't be able to tell the difference.

Did you know that cardamom was the best antidote for bad breath? Didn't think so. It is.
~~~~~~

Pyromania (aka Mexican) Hot Chocolate

- 1 cup / 8 fl. oz. milk of your choice (see ingredients page 8)
- ½ cup / 4 fl. oz. thick coconut milk
- 2 TBSP unsweetened cocoa powder
- 2 TBSP xylitol or erythritol (or sweetener of choice – see page 9)
- 3 tsp. vanilla extract
- ½ tsp. ground cinnamon
- ¼ tsp. ground cayenne

Place the milk, thick coconut milk, cocoa powder, xylitol or erythritol, vanilla extract, ground cinnamon, and ground cayenne in a pan and whisk well over medium heat until it starts to steam.

Remove from the heat and while it is still in the pan, whisk the hot chocolate using a handheld frother or immersion blender.

Serve with a squirt of fire extinguisher on the side.

Spicy Hot Chocolate

- 1 cup / 8 fl. oz. almond milk
- ½ TBSP unsweetened cocoa powder
- 2 TBSP xylitol or erythritol (or sweetener of choice – see page 9)
- 1 tsp. vanilla extract
- ⅛ tsp. ground cayenne
- ½ tsp. ground cardamom
- pinch of sea salt
- 2 oz. / 55g 100% unsweetened chocolate, chopped

Place the almond milk, cocoa powder, xylitol or erythritol, vanilla extract, ground cayenne, ground cardamom, and sea salt in a pan and whisk well over medium heat until it starts to steam.

Turn off the heat and add the chopped chocolate, stirring until completely melted and mixed through.

While it is still in the pan, whisk the hot chocolate using a handheld frother or immersion blender, then serve.

~~~~~~

Wildman – "Ooooh! That's got a kick!"

Since I have a spicy hot tolerance of minus 1, I won't be making these again. Just know that I went through the pain barrier to craft these two for you. You're welcome. You're worth it.
~~~~~~

Roasted Cocoa Bean Latte

- 2 TBSP roasted ground cocoa beans (brewing cocoa) *
- 1 cup / 8 fl. oz. boiling water
- ½ cup / 4 fl. oz. milk of your choice (see ingredients page 8)
- Xylitol or erythritol (or sweetener of choice – see page 9)

Brew the roasted ground coffee beans in a French Press or pan (saucepan) as you would coffee grounds. Brew for 10 – 12 minutes for fullest flavor. Pour brew into your cup, add sweetener and stir well. Add warmed and frothed milk (see page 14) as if you were making a regular latte.

Top with sugar-free marshmallows (page 73) – in which case you can omit the sweetener.

~~~~~~

* There are two brands of brewing cocoa available in the US at the time of writing – Crio Bru and Choffy. I do not know what is available outside the US, so I made my own by finely grinding cocoa nibs, which are available in most places.

If using cocoa nibs, grind them finely in a grinder that does not use heat (!) and then use 3 TBSP per cup / 8 fl. oz. of water.

Brewed cocoa beans do not give you a think, rich, chocolatey experience like the hot chocolate recipes in this section. It is like a coffee latte in texture and has a light, mild, mellow chocolate flavor. Perfect when you want a hot chocolate drink but don't want the thick, rich stuff.
~~~~~~

YOGURT & FROZEN DRINKS

Those perky baristas over at Starbucks do a rip-roaring trade in Frappuccinos and Smoothies, while cafés, ice cream parlors, and restaurant establishments across the world churn out milkshakes by the millions. Yep, we love our cold & frozen milk drinks. If only they weren't packed with enough sugar and high-fructose corn syrup to send a child into orbit for 3 hours or make your body rush headlong into fat-storing mode. In my "Eat Smarter! Ice Creams" cookbook I proved that you can still enjoy premium ice cream without any health downsides, so it had to be possible to create some cold & frozen milk drinks that hit the spot without sending you down the road to diabetes and heart disease.

Frappés are frozen coffee drinks that originated in Greece – they are simply iced coffee made with instant coffee. Of course, once they arrived stateside they morphed into chilled or frozen drinks – which either do or do not include coffee – and which usually include all manner of other ingredients such as large quantities of sugar, chocolate syrup, caramel...you get the picture. Mississippi Mud Pie Frappé, anyone? They are a lovely treat on a hot day, but since the ones available commercially are loaded with sugars and unhealthy fats, I figured we all needed healthy versions – all the taste with none of the health downsides.

NOTE* dandelion chicory blend = 1 tsp. roasted ground dandelion + 1 tsp. roasted ground chicory + pinch salt

Gingerbread Frappé

- 2 cups ice cubes
- 4 TBSP erythritol or to taste (or sweetener of choice – see page 9)
- ⅛ tsp. ground cinnamon
- ⅛ tsp. ground ginger
- pinch ground cloves
- ½ tsp. vanilla extract
- Pinch sea salt
- ¼ cup / 2 fl. oz. milk of your choice (see ingredients page 8)
- ½ cup / 4 fl. oz. COLD strong coffee or dandelion chicory blend * (see page 37)
- ¼ tsp. guar gum (optional – improves texture)

Place ingredients – except guar gum – in a blender and blend until ice is smooth. Tap the guar gum through the hole in the lid while blender is running and blend for 5 seconds.

No More Death By Chocolate Frappé

- 1 cup ice cubes
- 1 oz. / 30g 100% unsweetened chocolate, chopped
- 2 TBSP unsweetened cocoa powder
- 4 TBSP erythritol or to taste (or sweetener of choice – see page 9)
- 1½ tsp. chocolate extract
- 2 pinches of sea salt
- ½ cup / 4 fl. oz. milk of your choice (see ingredients page 8)
- ½ cup / 4 fl. oz. COLD strong coffee or dandelion chicory blend * (see page 37)
- ¼ tsp. guar gum (optional – improves texture)

Place ingredients – except guar gum – in a blender and blend until ice is smooth. Tap the guar gum through the hole in the lid while blender is running and blend for 5 seconds.

Pumpkin Pie Frappé

- 2 cups ice cubes
- ½ tsp. pumpkin pie spice
- 1 tsp. vanilla extract
- 4 TBSP erythritol or to taste (or sweetener of choice – see page 9)
- 3 TBSP pumpkin puree
- ½ cup / 4 fl. oz. milk of your choice (see ingredients page 8)
- ½ cup / 4 fl. oz. COLD strong coffee or dandelion chicory blend * (see page 37)
- ¼ tsp. guar gum (optional – improves texture)

Place ingredients – except guar gum – in a blender and blend until ice is smooth. Tap the guar gum through the hole in the lid while blender is running and blend for 5 seconds.

Grasshopper Fudge Frappé

- 1½ cups ice cubes
- ½ oz. / 15g 100% unsweetened chocolate, chopped
- 1 ½ tsp. chocolate extract
- ¼ tsp. peppermint extract (this stuff is *very* strong!)
- 1 tsp. caramel extract
- 3 TBSP erythritol or to taste (or sweetener of choice – see page 9)
- 1 TBSP unsweetened cocoa powder
- 2 pinches sea salt
- ½ cup / 4 fl. oz. milk of your choice (see ingredients page 8)
- ½ cup / 4 fl. oz. COLD strong coffee or dandelion chicory blend * (see page 37)
- ¼ tsp. guar gum (optional – improves texture)

Place ingredients – except guar gum – in a blender and blend until ice is smooth. Tap the guar gum through the hole in the lid while blender is running and blend for 5 seconds.

Hazelnut Mocha Frappé

- 2 cups ice cubes
- 3 TBSP erythritol or to taste (or sweetener of choice – see page 9)
- ¾ tsp. hazelnut extract
- 1 TBSP unsweetened cocoa powder
- ½ tsp. vanilla extract
- 2 pinches sea salt
- ¼ cup / 2 fl. oz. milk of your choice (see ingredients page 8)
- ½ cup / 4 fl. oz. COLD strong coffee or dandelion chicory blend * (see page 37)
- ¼ tsp. guar gum (optional – improves texture)

Place ingredients – except guar gum – in a blender and blend until ice is smooth. Tap the guar gum through the hole in the lid while blender is running and blend for 5 seconds.

Peanut Butter Cup Frappé

- 2 cups ice cubes
- ¼ cup smooth natural peanut butter
- ½ oz. / 15g 100% unsweetened chocolate, chopped
- ½ tsp. chocolate extract
- 3 TBSP erythritol or to taste (or sweetener of choice – see page 9)
- pinch sea salt
- 1 cup / 8 fl. oz. milk of your choice (see ingredients page 8)
- ¼ tsp. guar gum (optional – improves texture)

Place ingredients – except guar gum – in a blender and blend until ice is smooth. Tap the guar gum through the hole in the lid while blender is running and blend for 5 seconds.

Cherry Vanilla Frappé

- 1 cup ice cubes
- ½ cup frozen cherries
- 2 TBSP erythritol or to taste (or sweetener of choice – see page 9)
- ½ tsp. vanilla extract
- ½ tsp. cherry extract
- 2 pinches sea salt
- ½ cup / 4 fl. oz. milk of your choice (see ingredients page 8)
- ½ cup / 4 fl. oz. COLD strong coffee or dandelion chicory blend * (see page 37)
- ¼ tsp. guar gum (optional – improves texture)

Place ingredients – except guar gum – in a blender and blend until ice is smooth. Tap the guar gum through the hole in the lid while blender is running and blend for 5 seconds.

Raspberry Truffle Frappé

- 2 cups ice cubes
- ½ cup fresh raspberries
- 1 TBSP unsweetened cocoa powder
- 1 tsp. vanilla extract
- 1 tsp. chocolate extract
- ½ tsp. raspberry extract
- 3½ TBSP erythritol or to taste (or sweetener of choice – see page 9)
- 2 pinches sea salt
- ¼ cup / 2 fl. oz. milk of your choice (see ingredients page 8)
- ½ cup / 4 fl. oz. COLD strong coffee or dandelion chicory blend * (see page 37)
- ¼ tsp. guar gum (optional – improves texture)

Place ingredients – except guar gum – in a blender and blend until ice is smooth. Tap the guar gum through the hole in the lid while blender is running and blend for 5 seconds.

Coconut Frappé

- 1½ cups ice cubes
- ½ cup frozen unsweetened flaked coconut
- ½ cup / 4 fl. oz. thick coconut milk
- ¼ cup / 2 fl. oz. thin coconut milk
- 3 TBSP erythritol or to taste (or sweetener of choice – see page 9)
- ½ cup / 4 fl. oz. COLD strong coffee or dandelion chicory blend * (see page 37)
- ¼ tsp. guar gum (optional – improves texture)

Place ingredients – except guar gum – in a blender and blend until ice is smooth. Tap the guar gum through the hole in the lid while blender is running and blend for 5 seconds.

Caramel Pear Frappé

- 1½ cups ice
- 1 tsp. caramel extract
- 1 tsp. pear extract
- 2 TBSP erythritol or to taste (or sweetener of choice – see page 9)
- ¼ cup / 2 fl. oz. milk of your choice (see ingredients page 8)
- ½ cup / 4 fl. oz. COLD strong coffee or dandelion chicory blend * (see page 37)
- ¼ tsp. guar gum (optional – improves texture)

Place ingredients – except guar gum – in a blender and blend until ice is smooth. Tap the guar gum through the hole in the lid while blender is running and blend for 5 seconds.

Everyone's heard of Caramel Apples, but Caramel Pears? YUM.

Rose Cream Green Tea Frappé

- 2 cups ice
- 1 TBSP rose water
- ¼ cup / 2 fl. oz. milk of your choice (see ingredients page 8)
- 2 TBSP erythritol or to taste (or sweetener of choice – see page 9)
- ½ cup / 4 fl. oz. water brewed with 4 green tea bags, left to get cold

Place ingredients in a blender in the order listed and blend until ice is smooth.

Pineapple Mint Green Tea Frappé

- 1 cup ice cubes
- 2 TBSP erythritol or to taste (or sweetener of choice – see page 9)
- ½ cup / 4 fl. oz. frozen unsweetened pineapple pieces
- 8 fresh mint leaves
- pinch sea salt
- 1 cup / 8 fl. oz. water brewed with 4 green tea bags, left to get cold

Place ingredients in a blender in the order listed and blend until ice is smooth.

Maple Coconut Green Tea Frappé

- 2 cups ice
- ½ cup thick coconut milk
- 2 TBSP erythritol or to taste (or sweetener of choice – see page 9)
- 1½ tsp. maple extract
- ½ tsp. coconut extract
- ½ cup / 4 fl. oz. water brewed with 4 green tea bags, left to get cold

Place ingredients in a blender in the order listed and blend until ice is smooth.

Apple Pie Green Tea Frappé

- 2 cups ice cubes
- 2½ TBSP erythritol or to taste (or sweetener of choice – see page 9)
- ¾ tsp. pumpkin pie spice
- Half Granny Smith apple, cored and roughly chopped
- ¾ cup / 6 fl. oz. water brewed with 4 green tea bags, left to get cold

Place ingredients in a blender in the order listed and blend until ice is smooth.

Who knew green tea could taste so freakin' good?!

Orange Creamsicle Green Tea Frappé

- 2 cups ice cubes
- 3 TBSP erythritol or to taste (or sweetener of choice – see page 9)
- Half large orange, peeled
- 1 cup / 8 fl. oz. whole milk or nut milk of choice (see ingredients page 8)
- ½ cup / 4 fl. oz. water brewed with 4 green tea bags, left to get cold

Place ingredients in a blender in the order listed and blend until ice is smooth.

Raspberry Cream Green Tea Frappé

- 2 cups ice cubes
- 2 TBSP erythritol or to taste (or sweetener of choice – see page 9)
- ½ cup fresh raspberries
- ¼ cup / 2 fl. oz. plain unsweetened yogurt
- pinch sea salt
- ½ cup / 4 fl. oz. water brewed with 4 green tea bags, left to get cold

Place ingredients in a blender in the order listed and blend until ice is smooth.

Lemon Ginger Green Tea Frappé

- 2 cups ice cubes
- 2½ TBSP erythritol or to taste (or sweetener of choice – see page 9)
- ½ tsp. ginger extract
- 1 tsp. lemon extract
- pinch salt
- ½ cup / 4 fl. oz. water brewed with 4 green tea bags, left to get cold

Place ingredients in a blender in the order listed and blend until ice is smooth.

Green Tea Frappés have become my very favorite grown-up slushee. You need these in your life.

Lassis are a traditional Indian drink which is very simple – and so delicious! Lassi is the original drinking yogurt. I always loved a little bottle of drinking yogurt – those liquid, smooth, fruit-flavored yogurts at the store – but I stopped that habit years ago after I started reading labels and realized what was in them. If you – like me – miss your drinking yogurt fix, you will love lassi!

After I made the traditional version sugar-free (and after my mouth had stopped swooning) I headed online to see what was out there in the lassi department. I found 'lassi' recipes all over – except because this is America they are in reality more akin to sugar-laden milkshakes than a simple, healthy beverage. Sad but true. The internet is calling every milkshake-like thing that has yogurt in it lassi. Chocolate Nutella Lassi with Nutella, milk chocolate, and sweetened condensed milk, anyone? If you want the fruit, chocolate, and sugar-filled milkshake-style versions of 'lassi' then the internet is your friend. What you'll get here are simple recipes that let you increase your water intake in a delightfully delicious, refreshing, and health-boosting way.

Now, before you trot off to get your blender out, I just want to do a little refresher on buying yogurt.

Buy plain, unsweetened yogurt and compare brands to find the one with the least amount of sugar listed on the nutritional information on the back of the container.

These days, commercial yogurts are a minefield – many of them having more sugar in them than ice cream. Scary but true. So check your labels, and once you have found a brand with the lowest amount of sugar, stick with it. Otherwise you run the risk of thinking you're drinking a super-healthy lassi when it is actually loaded with sugar. UGH.

Lassis have become my absolute favorite drink. I have one every day.

Sweet Lassi

- ½ cup / 4 fl. oz. whole plain yogurt
- 1½ cups / 12 fl. oz. cold water
- 1½ TBSP xylitol or erythritol (or sweetener of choice – see page 9)
- 3 tsp. rosewater

Place all the ingredients into a blender and blend for 5 seconds. Pour into 2 glasses and serve.

Black Cherry Amaretto Lassi

- ½ cup / 4 fl. oz. whole plain yogurt
- 1½ cups / 12 fl. oz. cold water
- 1½ TBSP xylitol or erythritol (or sweetener of choice – see page 9)
- 1 tsp. cherry extract
- 1 tsp. almond extract

Place all the ingredients into a blender and blend for 5 seconds. Pour into 2 glasses and serve.

TMI: my saliva glands get going just thinking about downing a glass of this. Swoon.

Caramel Hazelnut Lassi

- ½ cup / 4 fl. oz. whole plain yogurt
- 1½ cups / 12 fl. oz. cold water
- 1½ TBSP xylitol or erythritol (or sweetener of choice – see page 9)
- ½ tsp. hazelnut extract
- ½ tsp. caramel extract

Place all the ingredients into a blender and blend for 5 seconds. Pour into 2 glasses and serve.

Strawberry Cream Lassi

- ½ cup / 4 fl. oz. whole plain yogurt
- 1½ cups / 12 fl. oz. cold water
- 1½ TBSP xylitol or erythritol (or sweetener of choice – see page 9)
- 1½ tsp. strawberry extract
- 1 tsp. vanilla extract
- pinch of sea salt

Place all the ingredients into a blender and blend for 5 seconds. Pour into 2 glasses and serve.

Pear Almond Lassi

- ½ cup / 4 fl. oz. whole plain yogurt
- 1½ cups / 12 fl. oz. cold water
- 1½ TBSP xylitol or erythritol (or sweetener of choice – see page 9)
- ½ tsp. pear extract
- ¼ tsp. almond extract

Place all the ingredients into a blender and blend for 5 seconds. Pour into 2 glasses and serve.

Apple Pie Lassi

- ½ cup / 4 fl. oz. whole plain yogurt
- 1½ cups / 12 fl. oz. cold water
- 1½ TBSP xylitol or erythritol (or sweetener of choice – see page 9)
- ¾ tsp. apple extract
- ½ tsp. cinnamon extract

Place all the ingredients into a blender and blend for 5 seconds. Pour into 2 glasses and serve.

Blueberry Maple Lassi

- ½ cup / 4 fl. oz. whole plain yogurt
- 1½ cups / 12 fl. oz. cold water
- 1½ TBSP xylitol or erythritol (or sweetener of choice – see page 9)
- 1 tsp. blueberry extract
- 1¼ tsp. maple extract

Place all the ingredients into a blender and blend for 5 seconds. Pour into 2 glasses and serve.

Apricot Cardamom Lassi

- ½ cup / 4 fl. oz. whole plain yogurt
- 1½ cups / 12 fl. oz. cold water
- 1½ TBSP xylitol or erythritol (or sweetener of choice – see page 9)
- ½ tsp. apricot extract
- 1 tsp. cardamom extract

Place all the ingredients into a blender and blend for 5 seconds. Pour into 2 glasses and serve.

Inspired by a donut in San Francisco, this is another favorite flavor combination. I just couldn't write a beverage cookbook without an Apricot Cardamom *something*. This is it.

Cranberry Spice Lassi

- ½ cup / 4 fl. oz. whole plain yogurt
- 1½ cups / 12 fl. oz. cold water
- 1½ TBSP xylitol or erythritol (or sweetener of choice – see page 9)
- 1½ tsp. cranberry extract
- ½ tsp. vanilla extract
- 1 tsp. cardamom extract
- ¼ tsp. cinnamon extract
- pinch sea salt

Place all the ingredients into a blender and blend for 5 seconds. Pour into 2 glasses and serve.

Perfect for the winter holidays! Thanksgiving and Christmas in a glass.

NOTE: you can use ground spices if you don't have extracts but you'll have a grainy feel to your lassi. The spices – especially cinnamon – do not dissolve in liquid. Smooth lassi is a very beautiful thing. (See pages 2 and 56 for information on extracts and flavors).

Mint Lassi

- ½ cup / 4 fl. oz. whole plain yogurt
- 1½ cups / 12 fl. oz. cold water
- ¼ cup fresh mint leaves
- ¼ tsp. salt
- ½ TBSP xylitol or erythritol (or sweetener of choice – see page 9)

Place all the ingredients into a blender and blend for 30 seconds. Strain into 2 glasses using a fine sieve and serve.

Coconut Lime Lassi

- ½ cup / 4 fl. oz. whole plain yogurt
- ½ cup / 4 fl. oz. thick coconut milk
- 1 cup / 8 fl. oz. cold water
- 1 TBSP xylitol or erythritol (or sweetener of choice – see page 9)
- ½ tsp. lime extract

Place all the ingredients into a blender and blend for 5 seconds. Pour into 2 glasses and serve.

THIS. IS. SO. GOOD!! Thicker than a traditional lassi and unbelievably delicious, says the girl who doesn't like coconut. Growing up coconut was one of three things I couldn't stand. The other two were spinach and melon. Now I eat more spinach and coconut than anything else. Truth.

SODAS, SPRITZERS, AND MOCKTAILS

I am guessing that this is the section that you lovely folks find the hardest to navigate from a health standpoint. For a lot of people, foregoing soda, pop, fizzy drinks, or whatever you call them in your part of the world, can be like trying to get pants on a fish. Growing up I almost never had them – they were a once a year treat over the Christmas holidays – so it wasn't like I was addicted to them by the time I reached adulthood. When I did reach adulthood and had the freedom to drink whatever I fancied, I didn't drink them because I didn't like all the bubbles. Then, out of the blue I discovered Dr. Pepper. I blame America since that's where I took my first sip. There was no looking back. Overnight I became a six-can-a-day girl, and not the diet kind either. Little did I know back then the disastrous effect it was having on me. Over the years I cut back, then switched to diet (yuck!) and finally landed on Cherry Coke Zero. Try as I might, I have found it nigh on impossible to totally kick it to the curb. I don't think I am alone in my love for soda. So I reckoned it was high time I figured out how to make healthy ones.

The main problem was getting sweetener into the mix that wasn't sugar or anything that is really sugar but called something else. I am looking at you, agave, honey, maple syrup, coconut sugar and a host of other substances touted as healthy. My go-to sweeteners, xylitol and erythritol, are notoriously difficult to dissolve in cold water, but with a few minutes of vigorous stirring or a quick buzz in the blender, all is well. Once I had that figured out, and thanks to my growing extract collection, the rest was fairly easy.

This is the section where I was challenged the most as a passionate cook – I wanted to make you artisanal, handcrafted sodas and mocktails made out of fresh herbs, spices, and fruits that would truly thrill your taste buds, but, and it's a BIG but, I also wanted you to have recipes that were practical in terms of time, effort, expense, and health benefits. Fruits – and juices in particular - contain a lot of sugars so they are not the best choice when it comes to beverages. From a time and effort perspective, the recipes in this cookbook can be thrown together in minutes, because I imagine that the majority of you are ridiculously busy with life and family and work, and really don't have time to make sage and basil syrups that are then downed in 10 seconds. So I made the decision to compromise on my make-it-all-from-scratch philosophy in order to give you drinks that were usable in real life on an ongoing basis. I will be posting some artisanal soda recipes over on www.carriebrown.com in the future, so that those of you who have the time, inclination, and passion can delve with me into that world.

This is also the section that I got most excited about once I got out of the starting blocks. I could have written a whole book just on sodas and mocktails. My head was just spinning with ideas left and right, and I had quite a time reeling myself back in so I wouldn't lose focus and go burrowing down a long and glorious rabbit hole instead. I stopped myself at just the basics for this book, but don't be surprised if there isn't an artisanal soda and mocktail cookbook somewhere on the horizon!

Like the lattes earlier in the book, I was stunned when I found out how simple making cocktails and sodas really is while the world would have us believe that they are something that only baristas, bartenders, and the clever commercial world can make. They are presented to us in a way that screams complicated! Secret recipe! Difficult to make at home! Flavors so complex you have no idea how we did it! Err, no. Not so.

While homemade sugar-free sodas seem like they must be really complicated (impossible?!) to make, they can be made really easily and quickly by using erythritol, extracts, citric acid, and plain sparkling water. Check out pages 2 and 56 to find out why I use extracts instead of fruits, herbs, and spices directly. Full disclosure: these sodas are not as sweet, thick, or syrupy as regular sodas.

If you look at some of these recipes and go, "Wow! That's a lot of sweetener!" bear in mind that the same amount of regular soda contains over 4 TBSP (12 tsp) of sugar and a Mojito packs about the same sugary punch. You can also adjust the sweetener amount to taste if they seem too sweet for you, but since erythritol is zero calorie and a zero on the glycemic index, it's OK;

These days I make up 2 liter bottles of soda from whichever recipe below is my current favorite so I don't have to stir up a glass every time I feel the urge to get fizzy with it. This is also a fabulous idea for day trips where you know full well there'll be nothing where you're going that won't make your pancreas think it's under siege. Ah, healthy soda – I love you.

Cream Soda

- 2 cups / 16 fl. oz. / 1 pint plain sparkling water
- 3 TBSP erythritol or to taste (or sweetener of choice – see page 9)
- 1 tsp. vanilla extract
- ⅛ tsp. citric acid

Put the ingredients in a glass or jug and stir vigorously until erythritol is dissolved.

Cherry Cola

- 2 cups / 16 fl. oz. / 1 pint plain sparkling water
- 4 TBSP erythritol or to taste (or sweetener of choice – see page 9)
- 1 tsp. vanilla extract
- ½ tsp. cinnamon extract
- ⅛ tsp. anise extract
- ¼ tsp. lime extract
- ¼ tsp. lemon extract
- ¾ tsp. cherry extract
- ¼ tsp. caramel extract
- ½ tsp. citric acid
- pinch sea salt

Put the ingredients in a glass or jug and stir vigorously until erythritol is dissolved.

Ginger Beer

- 2 cups / 16 fl. oz. / 1 pint plain sparkling water
- 3 TBSP erythritol or to taste (or sweetener of choice – see page 9)
- 3 tsp. ginger extract
- ¼ tsp. lemon extract
- ½ tsp. citric acid
- pinch sea salt

Put the ingredients in a glass or jug and stir vigorously until erythritol is dissolved.

Lemon Lime Soda

- 2 cups / 16 fl. oz. / 1 pint plain sparkling water
- 4 TBSP erythritol or to taste (or sweetener of choice – see page 9)
- ½ tsp. lemon extract
- ½ tsp. lime extract
- ½ tsp. citric acid
- pinch sea salt

Put the ingredients in a glass or jug and stir vigorously until erythritol is dissolved.

Black Cherry Soda

- 2 cups / 16 fl. oz. / 1 pint plain sparkling water
- 3 TBSP erythritol or to taste (or sweetener of choice – see page 9)
- 2½ tsp. cherry extract
- ⅛ tsp. citric acid
- pinch sea salt

Put the ingredients in a glass or jug and stir vigorously until erythritol is dissolved.

Strawberry Soda

- 2 cups / 16 fl. oz. / 1 pint plain sparkling water
- 4 TBSP erythritol or to taste (or sweetener of choice – see page 9)
- ¼ tsp. citric acid
- 1½ tsp. strawberry extract

Put the ingredients in a glass or jug and stir vigorously until erythritol is dissolved.

Orange Creamsicle Soda

- 2 cups / 16 fl. oz. / 1 pint plain sparkling water
- 4 TBSP erythritol or to taste (or sweetener of choice – see page 9)
- 2 tsp. orange extract
- ½ tsp. vanilla extract
- ¼ tsp. citric acid
- pinch sea salt

Put the ingredients in a glass or jug and stir vigorously until erythritol is dissolved.

Green Apple Soda

- 2 cups / 16 fl. oz. / 1 pint plain sparkling water
- 2 TBSP erythritol or to taste (or sweetener of choice – see page 9)
- ¼ tsp. vanilla extract
- ½ tsp. apple extract
- ¼ tsp. citric acid

Put the ingredients in a glass or jug and stir vigorously until erythritol is dissolved.

When I was young and my parents went to the pub for a tipple, I drank Appletise, which is a bright, fizzy apple juice. It was lovely, so I thought I'd make you some to try. GO, apples!

Licorice Soda

- 2 cups / 16 fl. oz. / 1 pint plain sparkling water
- 3 TBSP erythritol or to taste (or sweetener of choice – see page 9)
- ½ tsp. anise extract
- ¼ tsp. citric acid

Put the ingredients in a glass or jug and stir vigorously until erythritol is dissolved.

I could drink this stuff all day long. I just adore the flavor of anise. Or licorice. Whatever.

Root Beer

- 2 cups / 16 fl. oz. / 1 pint plain sparkling water
- 3 TBSP erythritol or to taste (or sweetener of choice – see page 9)
- ½ tsp. root beer extract

Put the ingredients in a glass or jug and stir vigorously until erythritol is dissolved.

Not Quite a Dr. Pepper

- 2 cups / 16 fl. oz. / 1 pint plain sparkling water
- 4 TBSP erythritol or to taste (or sweetener of choice – see page 9)
- ¾ tsp. raspberry extract
- ½ tsp. almond extract
- ½ tsp. vanilla extract
- ¼ tsp. caramel extract
- ½ tsp. cherry extract
- ¼ tsp. anise extract
- ¼ tsp. citric acid
- Pinch sea salt

Put the ingredients in a glass or jug and stir vigorously until erythritol is dissolved.

Lemonade

- 2 cups / 16 fl. oz. / 1 pint plain sparkling water
- 3 TBSP erythritol or to taste (or sweetener of choice – see page 9)
- 1 tsp. lemon extract
- ¼ tsp. citric acid
- pinch sea salt

Put the ingredients in a glass or jug and stir vigorously until erythritol is dissolved.

Margarita *(page 52 top left)*

- Large grain sea salt for glass rim
- 3 TBSP erythritol or to taste (or sweetener of choice – see page 9)
- 3 TBSP lime juice
- ½ cup / 4 fl. oz. water
- ½ tsp. orange extract
- ½ cup ice
- slice of lime to serve

Wet rim of glass and turn upside down into a plate of large grain sea salt to give the glass a salted rim. Add remaining ingredients into a cocktail shaker and shake for 30 seconds. Strain into a glass and garnish with a thin slice of lime.

Pina Colada *(page 52 top right)*

- ½ cup / 4 fl. oz. thick coconut milk
- ½ cup / 4 fl. oz. pure 100% unsweetened pineapple juice
- 2 cups ice
- frozen pineapple pieces to serve

Pour thick coconut milk and pineapple juice into a jug and stir well. Pour into 2 glasses over 1 cup ice in each and garnish with frozen pineapple pieces.

Cucumber Cooler *(page 52 bottom left)*

- 1 ½ English cucumbers, peeled
- 1 cup / 8 fl. oz. plain water
- 6 TBSP erythritol or to taste (or sweetener of choice – see page 9)
- ½ cup fresh mint leaves
- 1 lime, thinly sliced
- 3 cups / 24 fl. oz. sparkling water

Blend the cucumbers, plain water, and erythritol in a blender until completely smooth and then press through a fine mesh sieve. In a large jug muddle the mint leaves well, then add the blended cucumber, sliced lime, sparking water, and stir well. Serve over ice.

Pomegranate Spritzer *(page 52 bottom right)*

- 2 TBSP pure 100% unsweetened pomegranate juice
- 2 TBSP erythritol or to taste (or sweetener of choice – see page 9)
- crushed ice
- ⅓ cup / 6 fl. oz. sparkling water

Vigorously stir pomegranate juice and erythritol until completely dissolved. Pour into a glass over crushed ice and add sparkling water.

Cherry Limeade with Basil and Mint *(page 54 top left)*

- 4 TBSP erythritol or to taste (or sweetener of choice – see page 9)
- ¼ cup fresh basil
- ¼ cup fresh mint
- ½ cup / 4 fl. oz. pure 100% unsweetened tart cherry juice
- 1 tsp. cherry extract
- 3 TBSP lime juice
- 2 cups / 16 fl. oz. / 1 pint plain sparkling water
- frozen cherries, strips of lime zest to serve

Put the erythritol, basil, and mint in a jug and muddle the leaves well. Add the cherry juice, cherry extract, lime juice and sparkling water and stir well until erythritol is dissolved. Pour into glasses over ice. Garnish with a frozen cherry and strips of lime zest.

Mojitos *(page 54 top right)*

- 3 TBSP lime juice
- 8 large mint leaves
- 3 TBSP erythritol or to taste (or sweetener of choice – see page 9)
- sparking water
- 1 cup ice
- lime wedges, sprig of mint to serve

Add the line juice, mint leaves, erythritol, and 4 TBSP of the water to tall glass and muddle the mint leaves very well. Stir well and then add the ice. Fill the glass with plain sparking water. Garnish with lime wedges and a sprig of mint.

Moscow Mule *(page 54 bottom left)*

- 2 TBSP lime juice
- 1 TBSP erythritol or to taste (or sweetener of choice – see page 9)
- ½ cup / 4 fl. oz. Ginger Beer (page 49)
- ¼ cup / 2 fl. oz. sparkling water
- ice, lime wedge, ginger slice to serve

Add all liquid ingredients to a jug and stir vigorously until erythritol is dissolved. Pour into two glasses over ice and garnish each with a lime wedge and slice of fresh ginger.

~~~~~~

The first time I had a Mojito was just 3 months prior to this book being published. I took a lovely friend out for a birthday dinner, ordered up "Exciting non-alcoholic drinks, please!" and two Mojitos appeared a few minutes later. I declared right then and there at the table that I needed to write a healthy beverage book so that I could have Mojitos whenever I wanted. Oh my delicious! That mint! That lime! Even better - all the sweetness but none of the sugar rush.
~~~~~~

Cosmo *(page 54 bottom right)*

- 6 tsp. pure 100% unsweetened cranberry juice
- 5 TBSP water
- 2 TBSP lime juice
- ¼ tsp. orange extract
- 5 tsp. erythritol or to taste (or sweetener of choice – see page 9)
- crushed ice
- cranberries, orange zest to serve

Add all liquid ingredients to a jug and stir vigorously until erythritol is dissolved. Pour into two glasses over crushed ice and garnish each with cranberries and thin strips of orange zest.

~~~~~~

Extracts, Flavors and the Whole '*Natural*' Thing

Writing this cookbook has tossed a bunch of learning curves at me – all of them rather thrilling to my mad cooking scientist brain. Perhaps the biggest and funnest was learning about extracts. Most of these recipes use them, so I dug deep and studied up. You may have felt all queasy when you first saw all the extracts used herein, but never fear lovely readers! I am not going to encourage you to use something that turns out to be horrible for your health. That would be counter-productive. Not to mention stoopid.

It seems to me there's always been a bit of negative chatter about extracts and flavors – along the lines of *chemicals, artificial, additives* and other things that go bump in the night. So I did some research because I wanted to make sure that what I was using was indeed *natural* – I mean *really* *natural*, and they weren't just bandying the word around like you see on so many other foodstuffs these days. We all laugh and shake our heads when we see *"natural"* on the packet, never believing for one second that it was actually made from anything found in nature.

Well, it turns out that the only time the use of the word *"natural"* is regulated is with extracts and flavors. So when you read *"natural"* on any other type of foodstuff it may mean exactly nothing, but when it comes to extracts and flavors *"natural"* means that it truly is natural. It must be, and I quote: *"derived from a spice, fruit or fruit juice, vegetable or vegetable juice, edible yeast, herb, bark, bud, root, leaf or similar plant material, meat, seafood, poultry, eggs, dairy products, or fermentation products."*

So there you have it. You can use *"natural"* extracts with abandon, even if the extract ingredients list *"natural flavors"* as some of them do. If the bottle says *"imitation"*, *"artificial"* or *"added flavors"* without the use of the word *"natural"*, don't buy it. Just say no!

See? This is not just a cookbook – it's a mine of information ☺
~~~~~~

INFUSED WATERS

The Basics

I am certain that I don't need to wax lyrical about the health benefits of drinking water. You all know that water is the bomb when it comes to hydrating your body and the myriad associated benefits of that. The downside to water is that it's boring. B-O-R-I-N-G. If I am going to drink any appreciable quantity of the stuff, it needs to taste better than what comes out of the tap or bottle. Enter infused waters.

Infused waters are simply water that has fruits, vegetables, spices, or herbs added to it. As those gems of Mother Nature steep in the water they release their flavors, giving you a delicious glass of water with added nutrition. Think vitamin water that is actually full of vitamins but costs way less and has no junk in it. They are simple to make and the options are endless.

Here are some general tips and tricks to get started. There are added tips on the recipe pages specific to each.

- The recipes that follow are based on 4 pints / 8 cups / 2 quarts / 64 oz. water.
- Don't worry much about the ratio of fruits and herbs to water. This is not a science. Over time you will learn what flavors you like more or less of in your water. If you want a faster infusion that you will drink quickly, or like more potent flavors, add more fruits and herbs. If you intend to drink the infusion over a period of time, can wait for a slower infusion, or prefer a more subtle flavor, use less.
- Use whatever water you would normally drink to make your infusions. Tap, filtered, bottled – all work the same.
- Use cold or room temperature water for your infusions. Hot water will not only destroy vitamins and enzymes, but also makes your fruit look ugly and fall apart. No one wants ugly fruit, especially if you are serving infused water to guests.
- Put the water in the container first and then lower the fruits and herbs in.
- For iced waters, fill your container 1/3rd with ice, fill almost to the top with water and then lower in your fruits and herbs.
- A general guide to infusion times is 2 hours at room temperature or 4 hours in the 'fridge. Infuse the water in the 'fridge for 12 hours to get intense flavors. For infusions using only herbs and spices and no fruits or veggies, steep for 24 hours.

- If you have not drunk all the water after 18 hours of infusing fruits and veggies, remove the solids from the water.
- Store the infused waters in the 'fridge for up to 3 days after removing the solids. Un-refrigerated water containing fruits and veggies MUST be drunk on the day of infusion.
- Rinse your fruit, veggies, and herbs well using a soft brush before infusing. If you are worried about pesticides, rinse with a vinegar-water solution or peel your fruits and veggies prior to using.
- When using citrus fruits, remove the rind before infusing, or if you leave the rind on remove the citrus from the water after 4 hours of infusing. Citrus rinds make infused waters bitter if left too long.
- Fresh fruits generally release more flavor and juices into the water and do not fall apart as readily as frozen fruits, so use fresh whenever you can. When using fruits like pineapple, mango and watermelon, many grocery stores carry pre-cut fruit so you don't have to buy whole ones and drink pineapple or watermelon water for two weeks straight. Unless you really like pineapple or watermelon water, or have an awful lot of people over drinking infused water.
- Only use fresh herbs for infusing, never dried. Unless you want to drink water that tastes like dried grass, in which case, dried is the way to go. Some fresh herbs – such as rosemary – are very strong, so start with less and add more if necessary.
- When using leafy herbs like basil and mint, tear the leaves up before adding to the water as this will provide more flavor.
- Dried fruit doesn't result in great flavor so I don't recommend using them. Fresh is best when it comes to water infusions.
- If you want to re-use your fruits and herbs, add fresh water to the existing container of infused water when you have drunk half of it. Citrus are best for re-use. Soft fruits, not so much.
- You are far more likely to drink a lot of infused water if there is a large container on hand, so making it by the glass is not only labor intensive, but likely won't get nearly as much water inside you as making a large container that you can drink from all day.
- Large pitchers (jugs), large glass jars with lids, or glass beverage dispensers (the ones with the tap at the bottom) are all great choices for making infused waters in. You can also get special infusion pitchers which have a built in sieve to keep your solids separate from the water, making removal of the solids easy and making straining the water unnecessary. I prefer to have the fruits and herbs floating around, but each to their own.

The ingredients in these waters aren't just tasty and pretty, they also added nutrients to your glass. Here's some things they are reported to offer in health benefits. You can research each of them online, but here's some cliff notes to get you excited about introducing some new herbs and spices into your life.

Basil – packed with huge quantities of Vitamin A and Vitamin K and a whole host of other minerals, basil is good for cardiovascular health as well as protecting cell structure. An anti-inflammatory and anti-bacterial to boot.

Cardamom – my favorite spice is one of the most effective remedies against bad breath (who knew?!), fights tooth decay and gum disease, and has been shown to help with digestion and depression, as well as being packed with cancer-fighters and protecting the body against aging and stress. I knew there were reasons I love it so much!

Chamomile – an age-old medicinal herb used as a sleep aid, anti-inflammatory, allergy reliever, and digestive aid amongst a long list of other things.

Cinnamon – with reported health benefits ranging from blood sugar control to IBS and Candida relief, anti-oxidant and anti-fungal properties to lowering LDL cholesterol and triglycerides, cinnamon has been used for centuries as a medicine. Look for Ceylon Cinnamon instead of Cassia.

Ginger – very effective at alleviating digestive distress and relief from nausea along with anti-oxidant, very potent anti-inflammatory, and immune boosting properties. GO, ginger!

Lavender – antiseptic and anti-inflammatory, and thought to be useful for anxiety, insomnia, and depression. Also good for treating fungal infections and for wound healing.

Mint – most widely known for its relief of digestive distress, mint is also an anti-microbial and a source of vitamin C, manganese, and copper. Plus an anti-oxidant and anti-inflammatory.

Pomegranate – absolute chock full of anti-oxidants, pomegranate has been shown to lower blood pressure and cholesterol and increase the speed at which heart blockages melt away.

Rosebuds / petals – immune booster, skin moisturizer, body fat reducer, wound healer, and knee pain reliever are just some of the many benefits touted for the lovely rose. And you thought it was just for looking pretty and smelling nice.

Rosemary – stimulating your immune system, improving memory and concentration, aiding digestion, and increasing circulation. Rosemary is all that.

Sage – anti-oxidant, anti-inflammatory and improved brain function. Want some sage advice? Eat more sage – it will boost your wisdom quotient and improve your memory.

Thyme – used for centuries for chest and respiratory issues such as bronchitis, chest congestion, and coughs. Also shown to reduce cholesterol and blood pressure.

Vanilla – with anti-inflammatory, anti-oxidant, and anti-carcinogenic properties plus an abundance of B vitamins and minerals make vanilla a great choice and not just for its flavor.

Recipes are based on 4 pints / 8 cups / 2 quarts / 64 oz. water.

Strawberry Lemon Basil *(top left)*

- 8 medium strawberries
- 1 lemon
- ½ cup basil leaves

Hull and quarter the strawberries, slice the lemon thinly, and tear the basil leaves. Peel the lemon first to reduce bitterness if you are steeping for longer than 4 hours. Add to the water in your container and follow the infusing and storage tips on pages 57 and 58.

Cinnamon *(top right)*

- 4 cinnamon sticks

Simmer all the cinnamon sticks in 16 fl. oz. / one pint / 2 cups of water on the stove for 15 minutes. Let it cool and use as a concentrate to mix with the rest of the water in your container. Add the simmered cinnamon sticks. Follow the infusing and storage tips on pages 57 and 58. Side note: your house will smell fantastic!

Cardamom Chamomile Mint *(bottom left)*

- 2 TBSP cardamom seeds
- ½ cup dried chamomile flowers
- ½ cup mint

Lightly crush the cardamom seeds in a plastic sandwich bag using a rolling pin or similar object. Tear the mint leaves and add to the water in your container along with the crushed cardamom and chamomile flowers. Steep in the 'fridge for 24 hours to develop the flavors. Strain the water through a fine mesh sieve into a clean container and follow the storage tips on pages 57 and 58.

Cucumber Strawberry Lime *(bottom right)*

- ½ English cucumber
- 8 medium strawberries
- 1 lime

Slice the English cucumber thinly, hull and slice the strawberries lengthwise, and slice the lime thinly. Peel the lime first if you are steeping for longer than 4 hours to reduce bitterness. Add to the water in your container and follow the infusing and storage tips on pages 57 and 58.

Original
MASON

Recipes are based on 4 pints / 8 cups / 2 quarts / 64 oz. water.

Lemon Pomegranate *(far left)*

- 1 lemon
- ½ cup pomegranate seeds

Slice the lemon thinly, peeling it first to reduce bitterness if you are steeping for longer than 4 hours. Put the pomegranate seeds in the bottom of your container and gently crush with a muddler (or similar) to break the membranes. Pour the water into your container and add the lemon. Follow the infusing and storage tips on pages 57 and 58.

Vanilla Blackberry Rose *(middle left)*

- ½ cup blackberries
- 2 vanilla beans, sliced lengthwise and crosswise
- ¼ cup dried rose buds or petals

Place the berries in the bottom of your container and mash lightly with a muddler (or similar) to release some of the juices. Add the sliced vanilla beans and the rose buds to your container and fill with water. Follow the infusing tips on pages 57 and 58. After infusing, strain the water through a fine mesh sieve into a clean container and follow the storage tips on pages 57 and 58.

Black Cherry Vanilla *(middle right)*

- 1 cup black cherries
- 2 vanilla beans, sliced lengthwise and crosswise

Pit the cherries and cut in half. Add the cherries and sliced vanilla beans to the water in your container and follow the infusing and storage tips on pages 57 and 58.

Apple Cinnamon *(far right)*

- I red skinned apple
- 2 cinnamon sticks

Core the apple and slice very thinly. Immediately add the apple slices to cold water in your container to prevent them from browning. Add the cinnamon sticks and follow the infusing and storage tips on pages 57 and 58. This mixture will benefit from a longer infusion time. Remove from the 'fridge 1 hour before drinking as you get a lot more flavor than when drinking it straight from the 'fridge.

Recipes are based on 4 pints / 8 cups / 2 quarts / 64 oz. water.

Ginger Lime *(left)*

- 1 lime
- 2 pieces fresh ginger the size of your thumb

Cut the lime into small wedges, peeling it first to reduce bitterness if you are steeping for longer than 4 hours. Slice the fresh ginger finely. Gently squeeze the lime wedges in to the water in your container and then add the wedges and ginger. Follow the infusing and storage tips on pages 57 and 58.

Lavender Lemon *(right)*

- ½ cup dried lavender flowers
- ½ lemon

Place the lavender flowers with a small amount of water in the bottom of your container and mash lightly with a muddler (or similar). Finely slice the lemon, peeling it first to reduce bitterness if you are steeping for longer than 4 hours. Add the rest of the water and the lemon slices to your container, and follow the infusing and storage tips on pages 57 and 58.

Recipes are based on 4 pints / 8 cups / 2 quarts / 64 oz. water.

Raspberry Vanilla Lime *(left)*

- 1 lime
- 1 cup raspberries
- 2 vanilla beans, sliced lengthwise and crosswise

Finley slice the lime, peeling it first to reduce bitterness if you are steeping for longer than 4 hours. Place the berries in the bottom of your container and mash lightly with a muddler (or similar) to release some of the juices. Add the water to your container then add the lime slices and vanilla beans. Follow the infusing and storage tips on pages 57 and 58.

Raspberry Mint *(right)*

- 1 cup raspberries
- ½ cup fresh mint leaves

Place the berries and mint leaves in the bottom of your container and mash lightly with a muddler (or similar) to release some of the juices. Add the water to your container and follow the infusing and storage tips on pages 57 and 58.

Recipes are based on 4 pints / 8 cups / 2 quarts / 64 oz. water.

Rosemary Watermelon (*top)*

- 2 large slices of watermelon
- 1 sprig of fresh rosemary

Fill your container with water and add the watermelon slices and sprig of rosemary. Rosemary is strong so start with less and add more if necessary. Follow the infusing and storage tips on pages 57 and 58.

Cucumber Blueberry Basil *(middle left)*

- ½ English cucumber
- ½ cup fresh basil leaves
- ½ cup blueberries

Thinly slice the cucumber and tear the basil leaves. Place the berries in the bottom of your container and mash lightly with a muddler (or similar) to release some of the juices. Fill your container with water and add the cucumber and basil. Follow the infusing tips on pages 57 and 58.

Pineapple Mint *(middle right)*

- ½ cup fresh mint leaves
- 1 cup fresh or frozen pineapple chunks (unsweetened)

Tear the mint leaves. Fill your container with water and add the mint leaves and pineapple chunks. Follow the infusing and storage tips on pages 57 and 58.

Orange Cardamom Vanilla *(bottom)*

- 1 orange
- 1 TBSP cardamom seeds
- 1 vanilla bean, sliced lengthwise and crosswise

Slice the orange thinly, peeling it first to reduce bitterness if you are steeping for longer than 4 hours. Place the cardamom seeds in the bottom of your container with a small amount of water and mash lightly with a muddler (or similar) to release some of the oils. Fill your container with water and add the orange slices and vanilla bean. Follow the infusing tips on pages 57 and 58. After infusing, strain the water through a fine mesh sieve into a clean container and follow the storage tips on pages 57 and 58.

Recipes are based on 4 pints / 8 cups / 2 quarts / 64 oz. water.

Orange Chai *(left)*

- 1 orange
- 2 tsp. cardamom seeds
- 10 whole cloves
- 1 cinnamon stick
- ½ TBSP allspice seeds

Cut the orange into small wedges, peeling it first to reduce bitterness if you are steeping for longer than 4 hours. Place all the spices in the bottom of your container with a little water and mash lightly with a muddler (or similar) to release the oils. Fill your container with water and add the orange wedges. Follow the infusing tips on pages 57 and 58. After infusing, strain the water through a fine mesh sieve into a clean container and follow the storage tips on pages 57 and 58.

Peach Sage *(right)*

- 1 large peach, pitted
- ½ cup fresh sage leaves

Finely slice the peach and tear the sage leaves. Fill your container with water and add the peach slices and sage. Follow the infusing and storage tips on pages 57 and 58.

Recipes are based on 4 pints / 8 cups / 2 quarts / 64 oz. water.

Grapefruit Rosemary *(left)*

- ½ grapefruit
- 1 sprig of fresh rosemary

Cut the grapefruit into thin wedges, peeling it first to reduce bitterness if you are steeping for longer than 4 hours. Fill your container with water and gently squeeze the grapefruit wedges into it. Add the wedges and rosemary to the container and follow the infusing and storage tips on pages 57 and 58.

Citrus Cilantro (Coriander) *(right)*

- ½ lemon
- ½ lime
- Large bunch fresh cilantro (coriander)

Slice the lemon and lime thinly, peeling them first to reduce bitterness if you are steeping for longer than 4 hours. Place the cilantro in the bottom of your container and mash lightly with a muddler (or similar). Fill container with water and add the lemon and lime slices. Follow the infusing and storage tips on pages 57 and 58.

Recipes are based on 4 pints / 8 cups / 2 quarts / 64 oz. water.

Lemongrass Mint Vanilla *(top left)*

- 1 stalk lemongrass, finely sliced
- ¼ cup fresh mint leaves
- 1 vanilla pod, cut lengthwise

Place the sliced lemongrass and mint leaves in the bottom of your container with a small amount of water and mash lightly with a muddler (or similar) to release some of the oils. Fill your container with water and add the vanilla bean. Follow the infusing tips on pages 57 and 58. After infusing, strain the water through a fine mesh sieve into a clean container and follow the storage tips on pages 57 and 58.

Hibiscus Rose *(top right)*

- ⅓ cup dried rose buds
- 2 TBSP dried hibiscus flowers
- 1 TBSP rosewater

Place the rose buds, hibiscus flowers, and rosewater in your container and fill with water. Follow the infusing tips on pages 57 and 58. After infusing, strain the water through a fine mesh sieve into a clean container and follow the storage tips on pages 57 and 58.

Mandarin Blueberry Thyme *(bottom left)*

- ½ cup blueberries
- 3 mandarin oranges
- 3 sprigs fresh thyme

Place the berries in the bottom of your container and mash lightly with a muddler (or similar) to release some of the juices. Cut the mandarins into wedges, peeling first to reduce bitterness if you are steeping for longer than 4 hours. Add to your container with the thyme, and fill with water. Follow the infusing and storage tips on pages 57 and 58.

Pear Fennel *(bottom right)*

- ½ large fennel bulb, plus some fronds
- 1 pear, ripe but firm

Slice the fennel thinly. Quarter, core and thinly slice the pear. Fill your container with water and add the fennel and pear slices, plus some fennel fronds for decoration. Follow the infusing and storage tips on pages 57 and 58.

The Saga of the Syrups

Let's talk about sugar alcohols and the shenanigans I traversed to bring you a cookbook of sugar-free beverages. I jotted down the basics about xylitol and erythritol on page 10, but wanted to explain my decisions around which sweeteners to use in different recipes. It took a *LOT* of experimentation. Two months leading up to this tome being launched into the world my kitchen was filled with little round Pyrex dishes with varying combinations of xylitol, erythritol, glycerin, isomalt, and water in them. Varying concentrations cooked at various temperatures and in differing ratios. My kitchen island looked like a science lab with dishes spread out all over and increasing in number by the day. Each morning I would run excitedly downstairs to see what had transpired in the dishes overnight. What was my goal? A simple syrup to make getting sweeteners into things like soda and mocktails easy. Why? Because xylitol and erythritol are just not the easiest things to dissolve in cold water. I was bound and determined to make you syrup.

Enter the absolute bane of my cooking existence: crystallization. If xylitol is a bear when it comes to re-crystallization, erythritol is a whole herd of bears – or whatever bears come in – and big, black angry bears at that. You melt erythritol and almost before you can lift the pan off the stove it's re-crystallized. I read research papers and scoured the internet for days. I tried glycerin and isomalt and a multitude of other things to hinder crystallization but to no avail. I eventually found a way to do it, but the ratio of erythritol: water was so low that it wasn't sweet. Crazy. A syrup that wasn't sweet. So erythritol syrups were out. Drat.

All was not lost! I finally figured out how to make syrups with xylitol that didn't crystallize. NO CRYSTALLIZATION!! HURRAH!! There was a major amount of celebrating at this juncture. Cheers rang out. There was dancing around the kitchen island. Cats hid behind the couch. I had solved my crystallization crisis and had you a syrup that would make soda-making so easy. That day there was a very merry mad scientist in the kitchen.

Then as I excitedly went full-tilt into sugar-free soda production I made a very interesting discovery: when xylitol or xylitol syrup is used in a recipe that is essentially just water – such as soda, mocktails, and teas – the laxative effect of xylitol is way stronger. While I can eat loads of xylitol in foods or dairy drinks with no laxative effect at all, putting it in sparkling water for sodas had me jogging rapidly to the bathroom. I tested this theory out on my long-suffering beverage tester, Wildman. Same result – when he eats xylitol in ice cream, lassis, muffins, or anything else akin to them he has no ill effects. Bring on the sodas, frappés, teas, and mocktails, and he'd better have a clear path to the bathroom. So Xylitol syrups were out. In fact, xylitol was out altogether for water-based beverages. I cried.

The short story of this 2-month-long experiment is you'll have to use a bit of gumption to vigorously stir the water-based beverages until the erythritol dissolves. The other thing that is important to note is that even if you have been tolerant of xylitol up to this point, if you want to avoid a potential mishap involving the bathroom, use erythritol in the water-based drinks – don't swap it out for xylitol. The upside to erythritol is it has zero calories, zero effect on blood sugar and insulin, tastes almost exactly like sugar, and has no laxative effect. Score!

Sugar-free Marshmallows

¼ cup / 2 fl. oz. cold water

1 TBSP powdered gelatin

5 ¼ oz. / 150g xylitol

¼ cup / 2 fl. oz. hot water

¼ cup / 2 fl. oz. vegetable glycerin

1 tsp. vanilla extract

Powdered xylitol

Spray a cookie tray with coconut oil spray and set aside.

Put the cold water in a small dish and sprinkle the powdered gelatin slowly and evenly over the surface so that it dissolves in the water. Set aside.

Place the xylitol, hot water, and vegetable glycerin in a small pan over a high heat.

The xylitol will melt and become clear.

Gently add the softened gelatin to the pan and stir carefully until it has dissolved.

Once the gelatin has dissolved, allow the syrup to come to the boil.

CAUTION! MELTED XYLITOL IS RIDICULOUSLY HOT. Don't be scared, but PLEASE BE CAREFUL. (The boiling point of water is 100 °C. The boiling point of xylitol is 212 °C. That's hot.)

Carefully, and slowly to avoid splashes, pour the boiling syrup into a large glass mixing bowl, or the bowl of your stand mixer, if you have one.

Add the vanilla extract, and then whisk on HIGH – either in your stand mixer or with a hand mixer – for 15 minutes. Yes, 15 minutes. If you use a hand mixer you will start to hate me at about the 4 ½ minute mark because it will feel like 15 minutes already and you still have 10 ½ to go.

As you whisk, the syrup will transform into a white, fluffy meringue-like mass. After 15 minutes you will get stiff peaks, like meringue.

Transfer the marshmallow into a piping bag with a small plain nozzle in it. Pipe small blobs of marshmallow onto the cookie trays sprayed with coconut oil.

Lightly sieve powdered xylitol over the marshmallows, and leave to set for several hours. Store in an airtight glass container using greaseproof or waxed paper between the layers.

WHERE TO GET MORE COOL STUFF

CarrieBrown.com - Recipes! Recipes! Recipes!

Fat-burning, health-boosting, delicious goodness, with tips and tricks for living a super healthy, sane lifestyle.

SANESolution.com - Weight Loss 2.0: Eat more, burn more.

Based on 10 years of scientific research – information, podcast, resources and support group for those following a SANE lifestyle.

BurnFatNotSugar.com - Diet and Exercise 2.0: A Doctor's Guide.

What to eat and how to exercise to heal your body and turn it into a fat burning machine.

EatingAcademy.com - Dr. Peter Attia

Losing weight, reducing your risk of chronic disease (heart disease, cancer, diabetes, Alzheimer's...), and improving your performance (physically and mentally).

GaryTaubes.com

Why we get fat and what to do about it.

www.carriebrown.com

I am a Food and Lifestyle Blogger, Podcast Co-host, Recipe Developer, and Food Photographer who focuses excitedly and tirelessly on creating truly healthy, truly scrumptious recipes based on The Calorie Myth by Jonathan Bailor. I am devoted to using my ex-pastry chef talents to conjure up delicious recipes that can help the world eat and drink smarter, live better, and put the 'healthy' back into healthy again.

This is my fourth cookbook, joining "Eat Smarter! Ice Creams", "Eat Smarter! Soups", and "Eat Smarter! Smoothies and Sides" on the culinary bookshelf.

When I am not making stuff up in the kitchen you'll likely find me roaring around the country shooting landscapes and otherwise exploring this amazing world that we live in. I like life better when it's real, rambunctious, and slightly irreverent.

I have a humongous appetite, an accent like crack (apparently), and a love for people who keep on going when the going gets tough. I think leeks are the finest vegetables on earth, although beets and fennel are pretty close behind. I can't swim.

I love living in Seattle with a couple of large cameras, a ridiculous amount of cocoa powder, and a pile of cats – Florence, Dougal, Penelope, Zebedee, Daisy, and Mr. McHenry.

Lattes

Almond Mocha....20
Black Cherry Amaretto....18
Cardamom....17
Cinnamon Roll....17
Coconut Cream....22
Gingerbread....20
No Nutella Nutella....21
Peppermint Mocha....19
Pumpkin Spice....21
Raspberry Truffle....19
Salted Caramel....18
Vanilla Rose....22

Teas

Chai Indian Tea....28
Chai Tea Latte....24
Ginger Tea....25
Green Tea with Cardamom and Cinnamon....25
Herb Matcha Iced Tea....27
Hibiscus Tea....28
Matcha Mint Tea....27
Pomegranate Iced Green Tea with Lemon....27
Raspberry Mint Iced Tea....25

Hot Chocolates

Cardamom Hot Chocolate....34
Creamy Peppermint Hot Chocolate....33
Hot Chocolate like You've Never had Before....31
Pyromania (aka Mexican) Hot Chocolate....35
Roasted Cocoa Bean Latte....36
Spicy Hot Chocolate....35
Vanilla Cinnamon Hot Chocolate....32

Frappés (frozen drinks): Coffee-based

Caramel Pear Frappé....41
Cherry Vanilla Frappé....40
Coconut Frappé....40
Gingerbread Frappé....38
Grasshopper Fudge Frappé....39
Hazelnut Mocha Frappé....39
No More Death by Chocolate Frappé....38
Peanut Butter Cup Frappé....39
Pumpkin Pie Frappé....38
Raspberry Truffle Frappé....40

Frappés (frozen drinks): Green Tea-based

Apple Pie Green Tea Frappé....42
Lemon Ginger Green Tea Frappé....42
Maple Coconut Green Tea Frappé....41
Orange Creamsicle Green Tea Frappé....42
Pineapple Mint Green Tea Frappé....41
Raspberry Cream Green Tea Frappé....42
Rose Cream Green Tea Frappé....41

Lassis (yogurt drinks)

Apple Pie Lassi....45
Apricot Cardamom Lassi....45
Black Cherry Amaretto Lassi....44
Blueberry Maple Lassi....45
Caramel Hazelnut Lassi....44
Coconut Lime Lassi....46
Cranberry Spice Lassi....46
Mint Lassi....46
Pear Almond Lassi....45
Strawberry Cream Lassi....44
Sweet Lassi....44

Sodas

Black Cherry Soda....50
Cherry Cola....48
Cream Soda....48
Ginger Beer....49
Green Apple Soda....50
Lemon Lime Soda....49
Lemonade....51
Licorice Soda....51
Not Quite a Dr. Pepper....51
Orange Creamsicle Soda....50
Root Beer....51
Strawberry Soda....50

Spritzers and Mocktails

Cherry Limeade with Basil and Mint....55
Cosmo....56
Cucumber Cooler....53
Margarita....53
Mojitos....55
Moscow Mule....55
Pina Colada....53
Pomegranate Spritzer....53

Infused Waters

Apple Cinnamon....63
Black Cherry Vanilla....63
Cardamom Chamomile Mint....61
Cinnamon....61
Citrus Cilantro (Coriander)....69
Cucumber Blueberry Basil....67
Cucumber Strawberry Lime....61
Ginger Lime....64

Grapefruit Rosemary....69
Hibiscus Rose....71
Lavender Lemon....64
Lemon Pomegranate....63
Lemongrass Mint Vanilla....71
Mandarin Blueberry Thyme....71
Orange Cardamom Vanilla....67
Orange Chai....68
Peach Sage....68
Pear Fennel....71
Pineapple Mint....67
Raspberry Mint....65
Raspberry Vanilla Lime....65
Rosemary Watermelon....67
Strawberry Lemon Basil....61
Vanilla Blackberry Rose....63

Additions

Sugar-free Marshmallows....73

Useful Info

Ingredients....5
Equipment....11
Latte How-To....13
Tea Tips....23
Chocolate and Cocoa Choices....29
What is a Frappé?....37
What is a Lassi?....43
How healthy sodas and mocktails are easy....47
Extracts & Flavors: Natural or not?....56
Infused Waters: The Basics + nutrition....57
The Saga of The Syrups....72

41920675R00051

Made in the USA
Lexington, KY
01 June 2015